Any Sunday In Coacalco

Tyler Blint-Welsh

Blurring Books

with a question. Often, it's one I can't answer. Once the question was:

What's it like at a backyard wrestling match in Mexico?

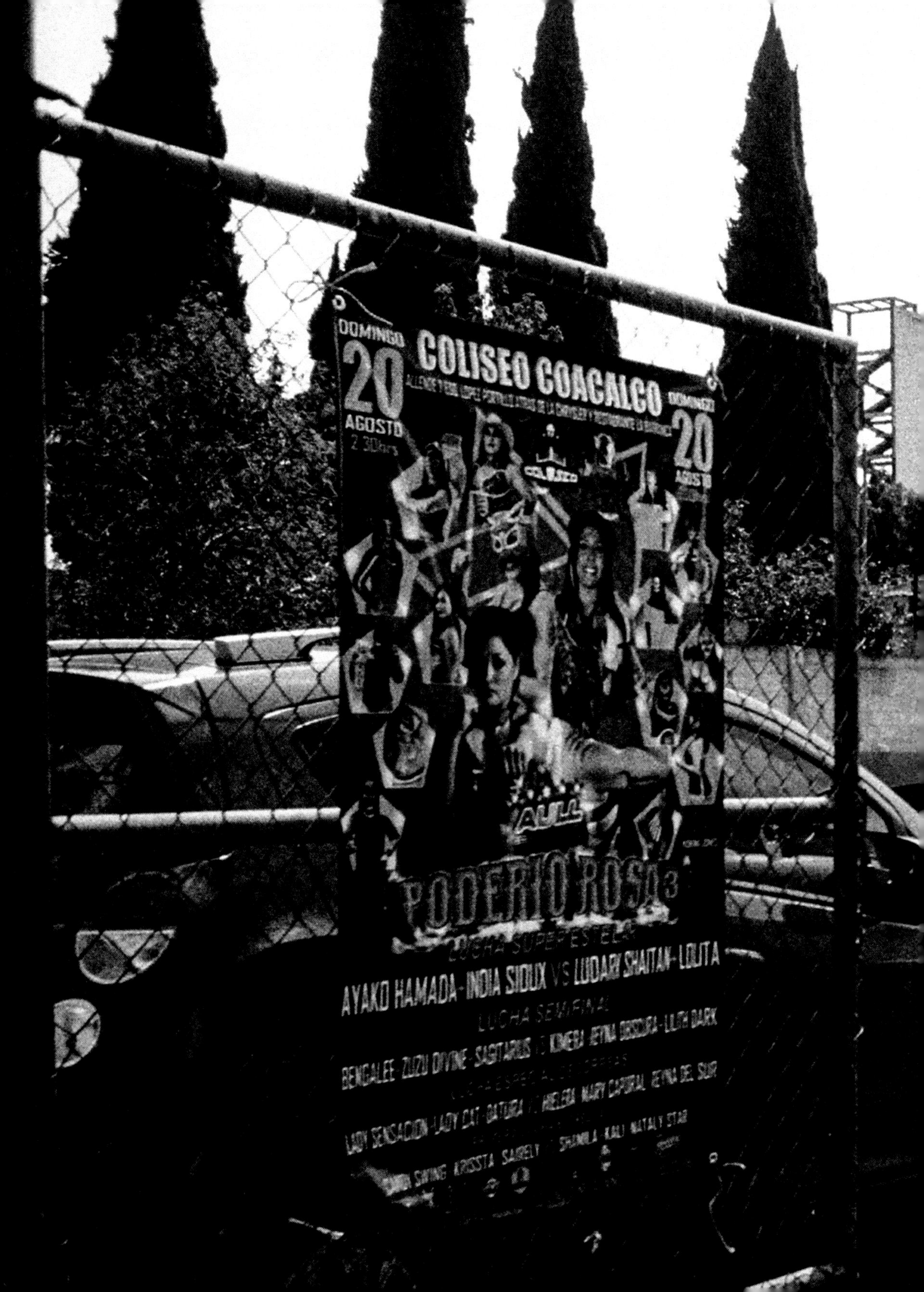

DOMINGO
20
AGOSTO
COLISEO COACALCO
DOMINGO
20
AGOSTO
PODERIO ROSA 3
LUCHA SUPERESTELAR
AYAKO HAMADA - INDIA SIOUX VS LUDARK SHAITAN - LOLITA
LUCHA SEMIFINAL
BENGALEE - ZUZU DIVINE - SAGITARIUS VS KIMERA - REYNA OBSCURA - LILITH DARK

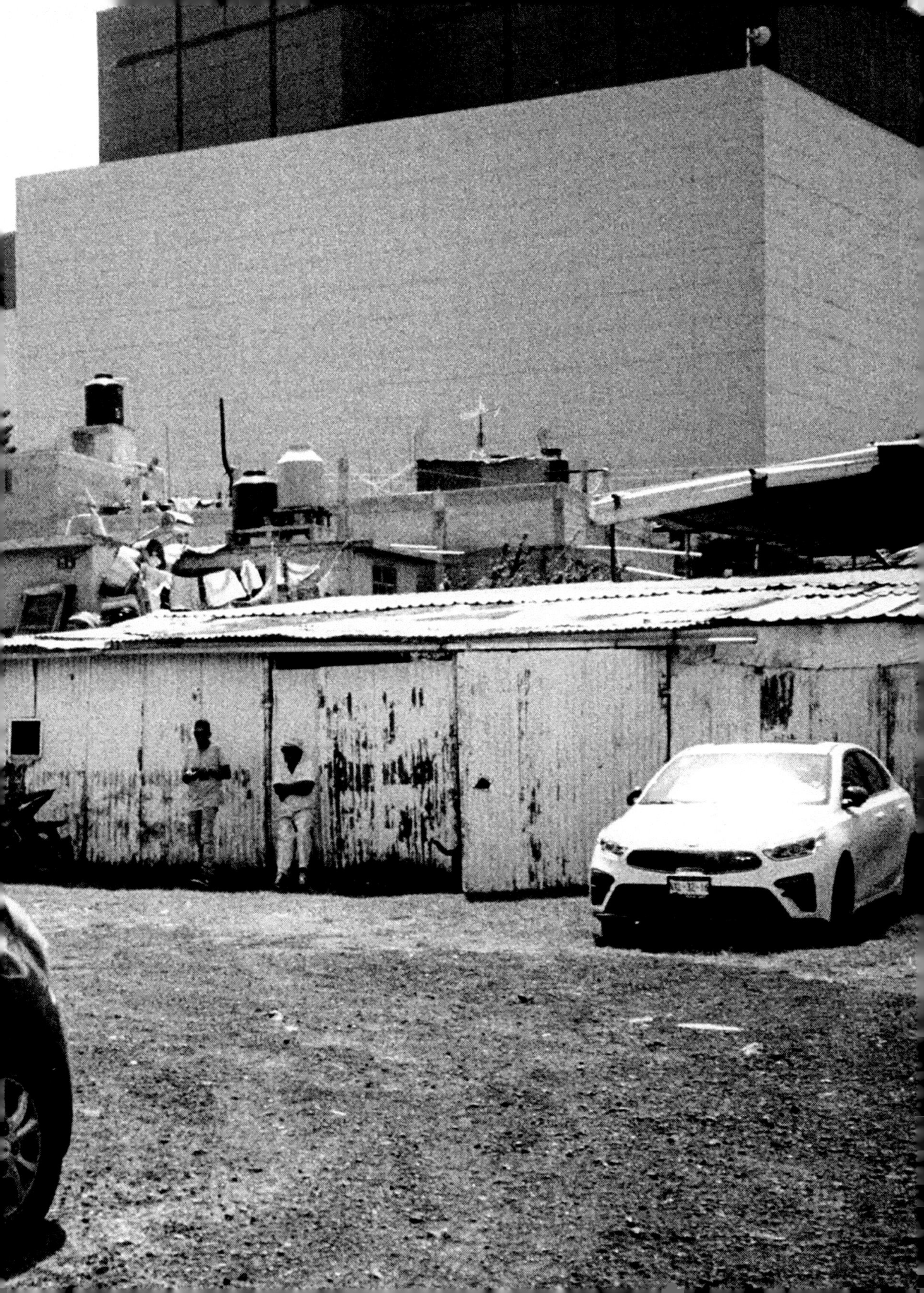

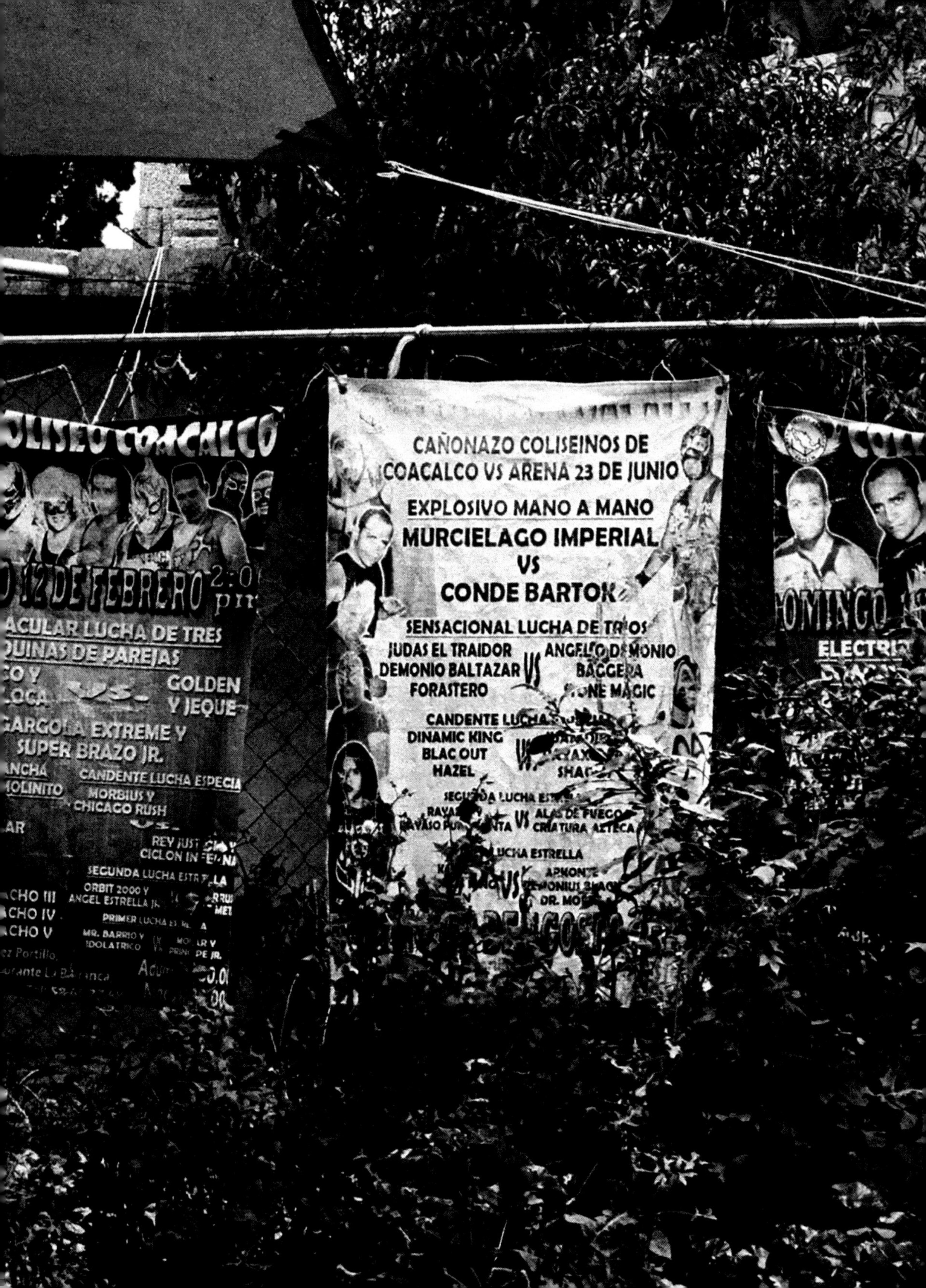
12 DE FEBRERO
GOLDEN
Y JEQUE
SUPER BRAZO JR.
MORBIUS Y
CHICAGO RUSH
ORBIT 2000 Y
MR. BARRIO Y
CAÑONAZO COLISEINOS DE
COACALCO VS ARENA 23 DE JUNIO
EXPLOSIVO MANO A MANO
MURCIELAGO IMPERIAL
VS
CONDE BARTOK
JUDAS EL TRAIDOR
DEMONIO BALTAZAR
FORASTERO
VS
DINAMIC KING
BLAC OUT
HAZEL
LUCHA ESTRELLA

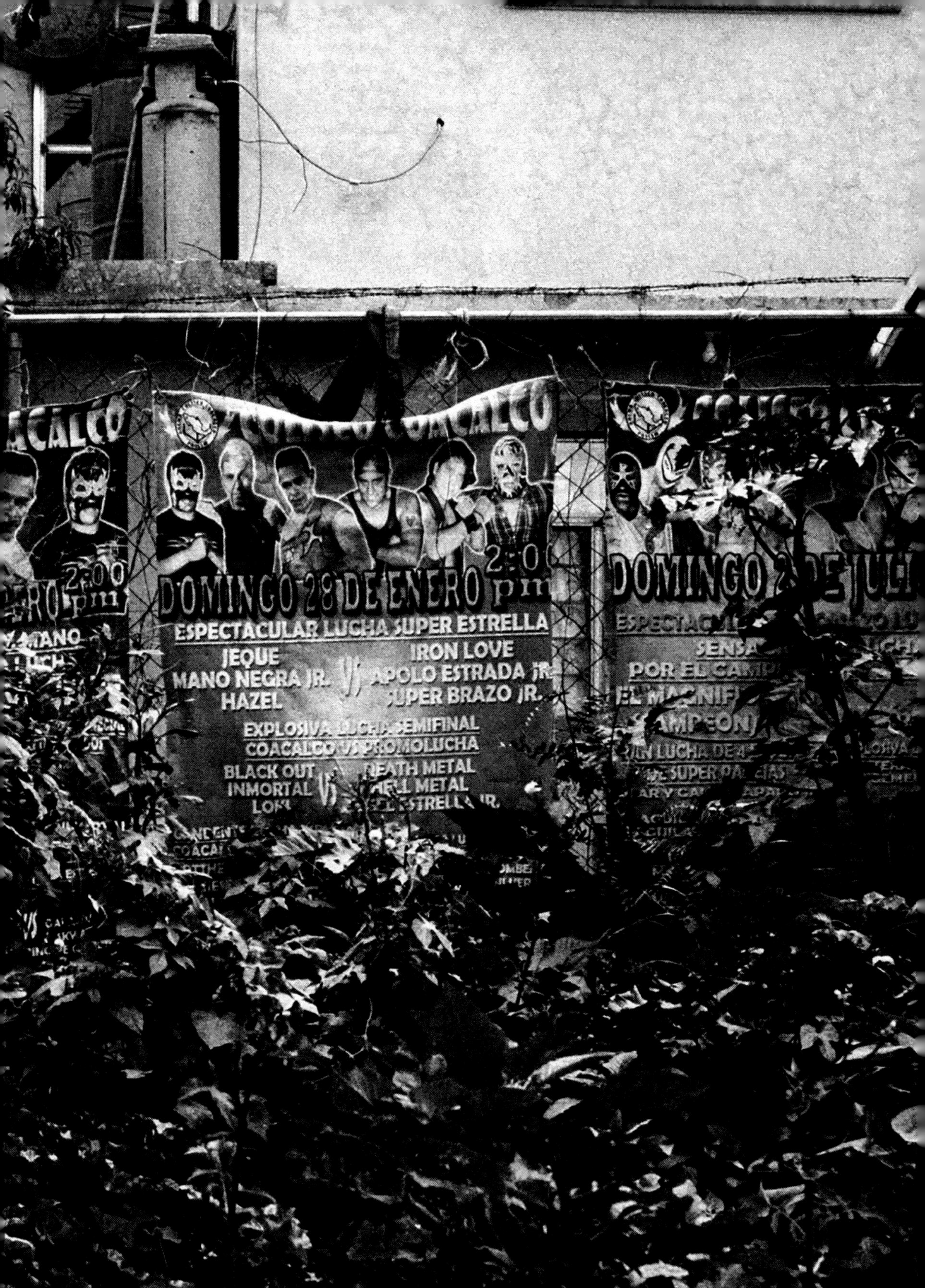

2:00 pm
DOMINGO 28 DE ENERO
ESPECTACULAR LUCHA SUPER ESTRELLA
JEQUE
MANO NEGRA JR.
HAZEL
VS
IRON LOVE
APOLO ESTRADA JR.
SUPER BRAZO JR.
COACALCO VS PROMOLUCHA
BLACK OUT
INMORTAL
DEATH METAL
HELL METAL

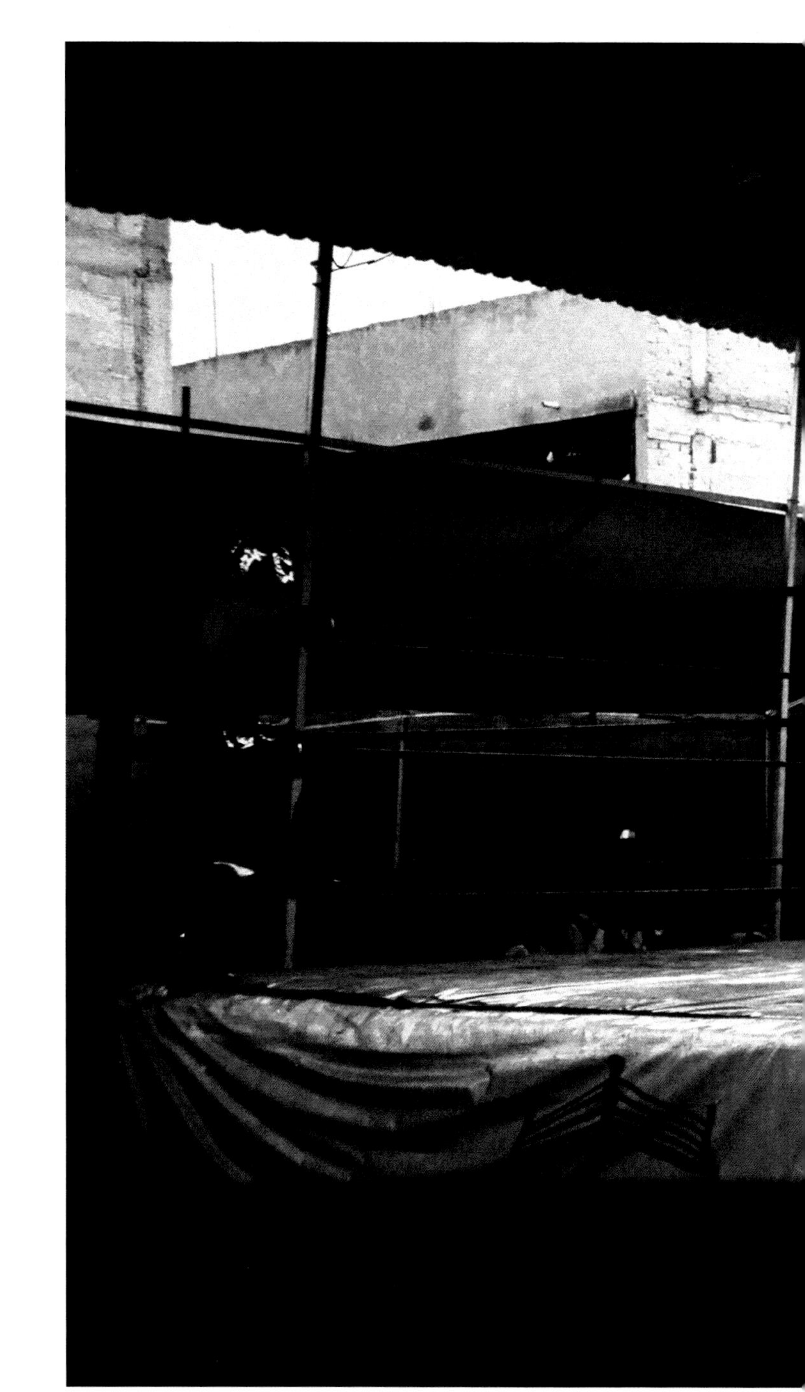

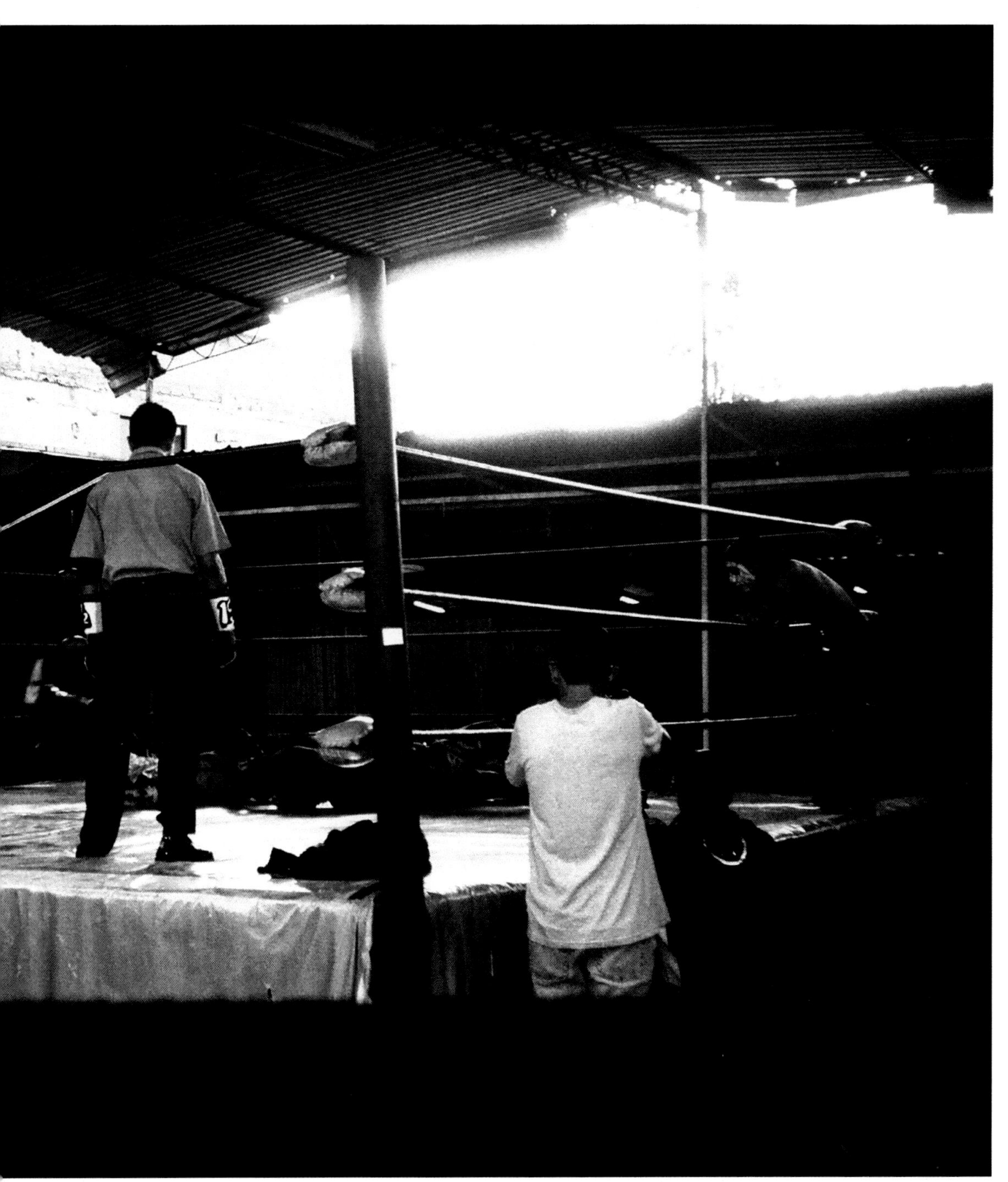

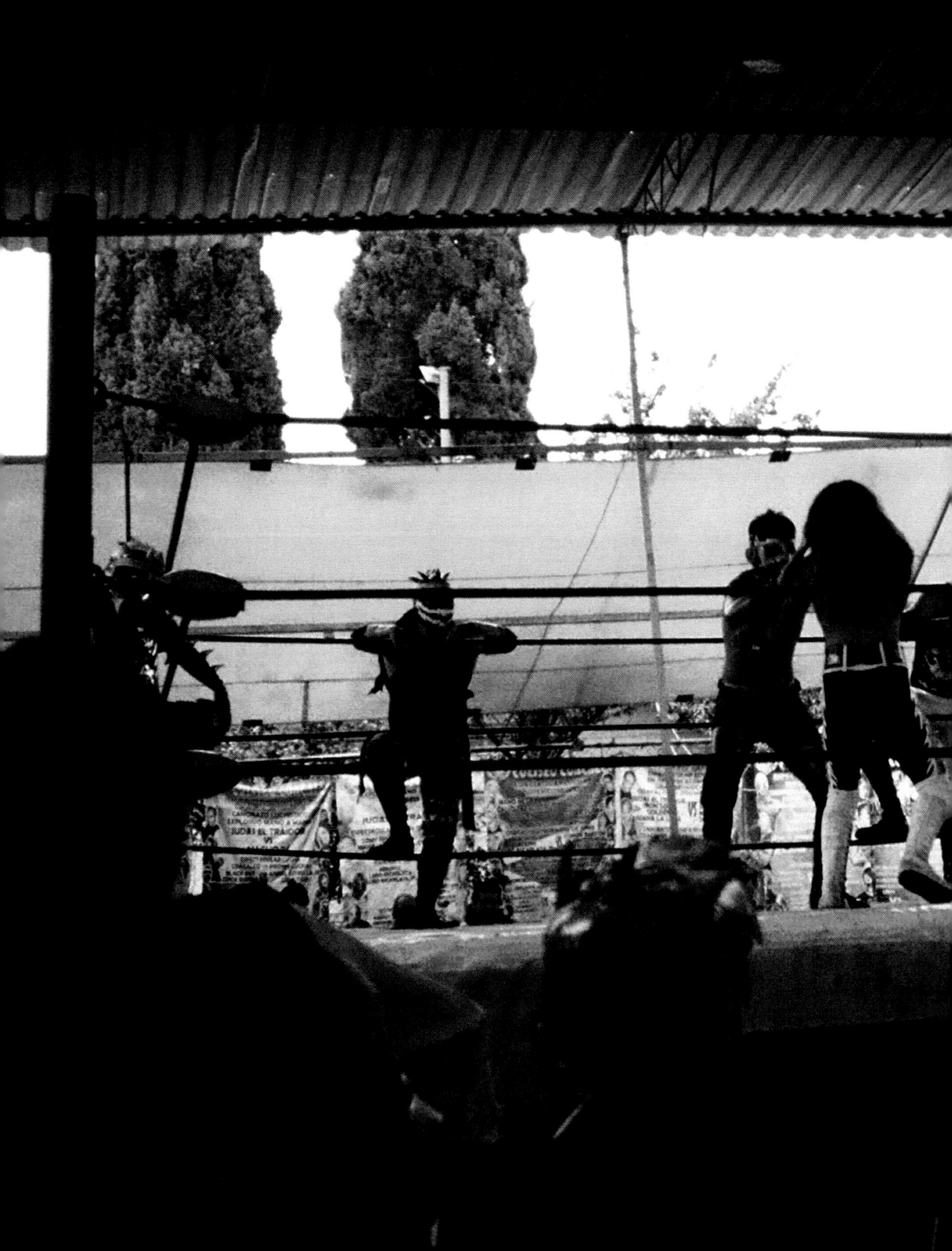

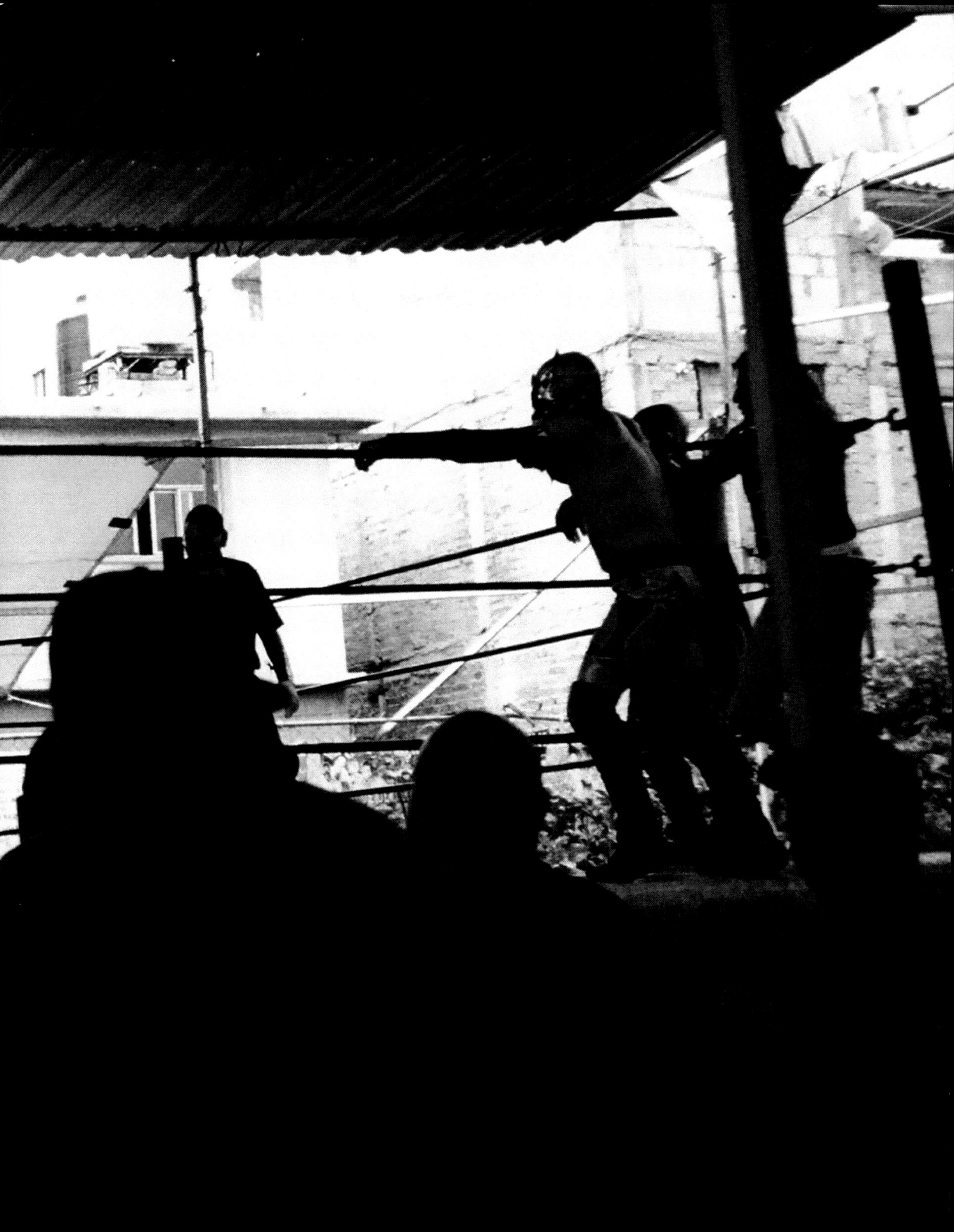

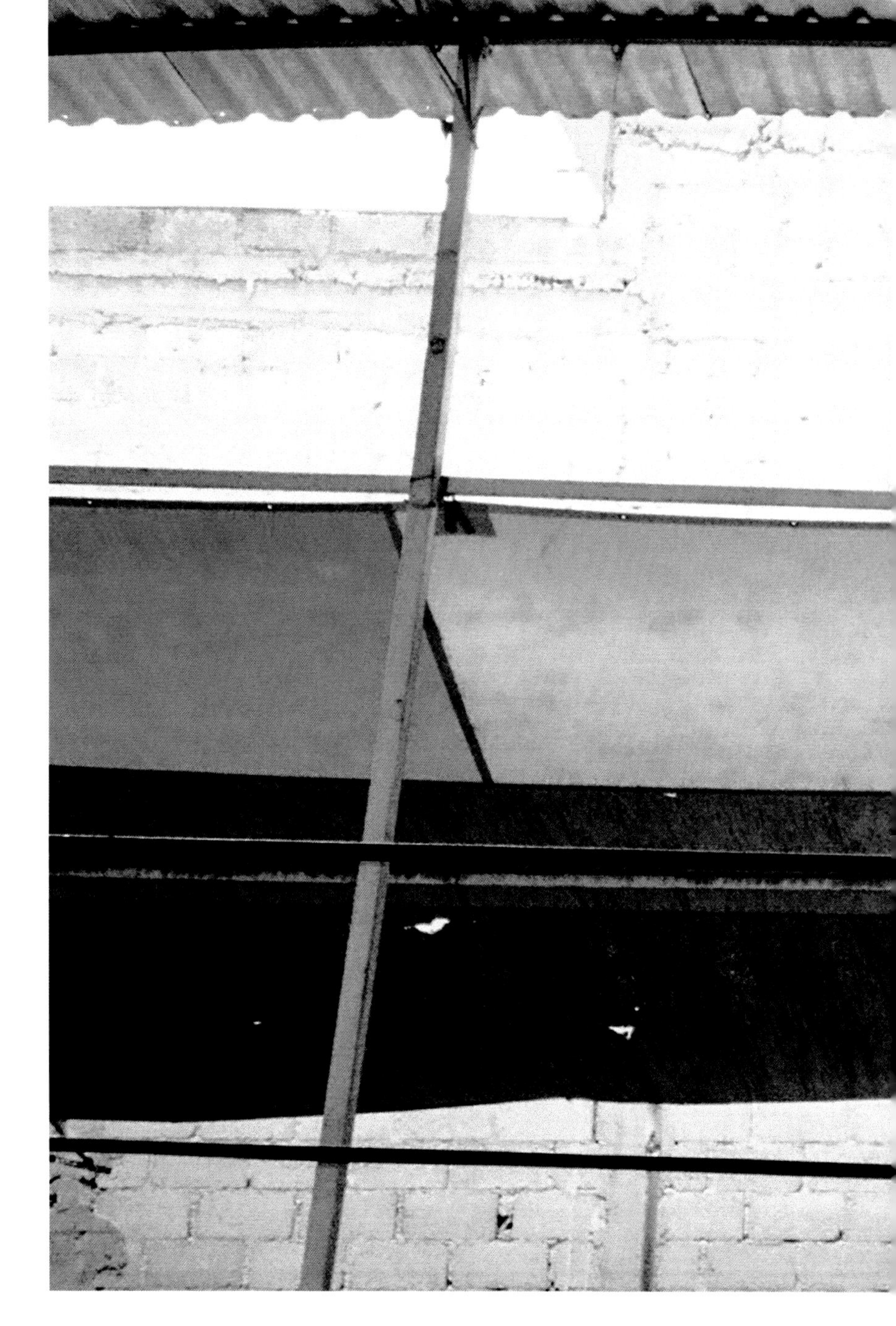

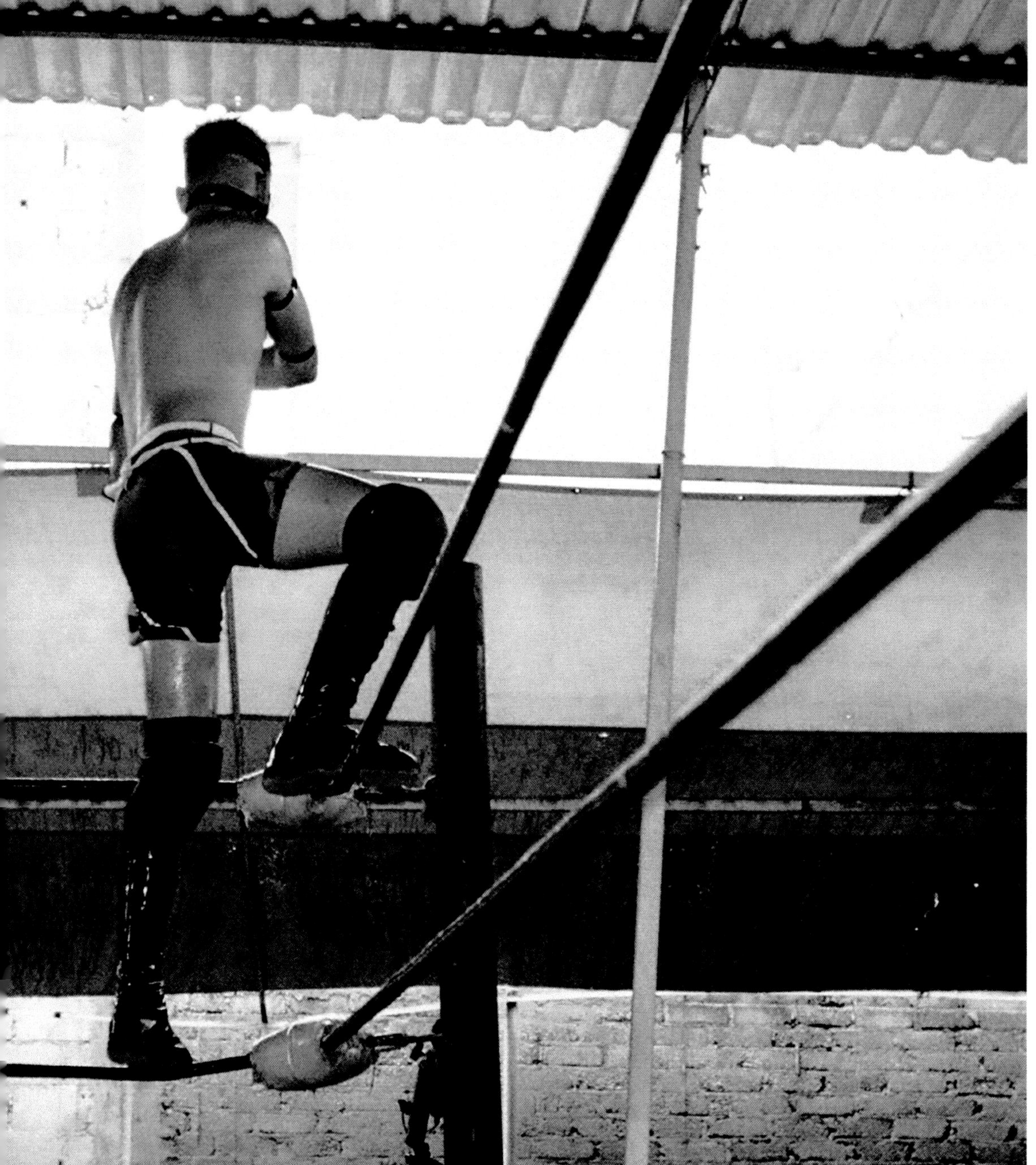

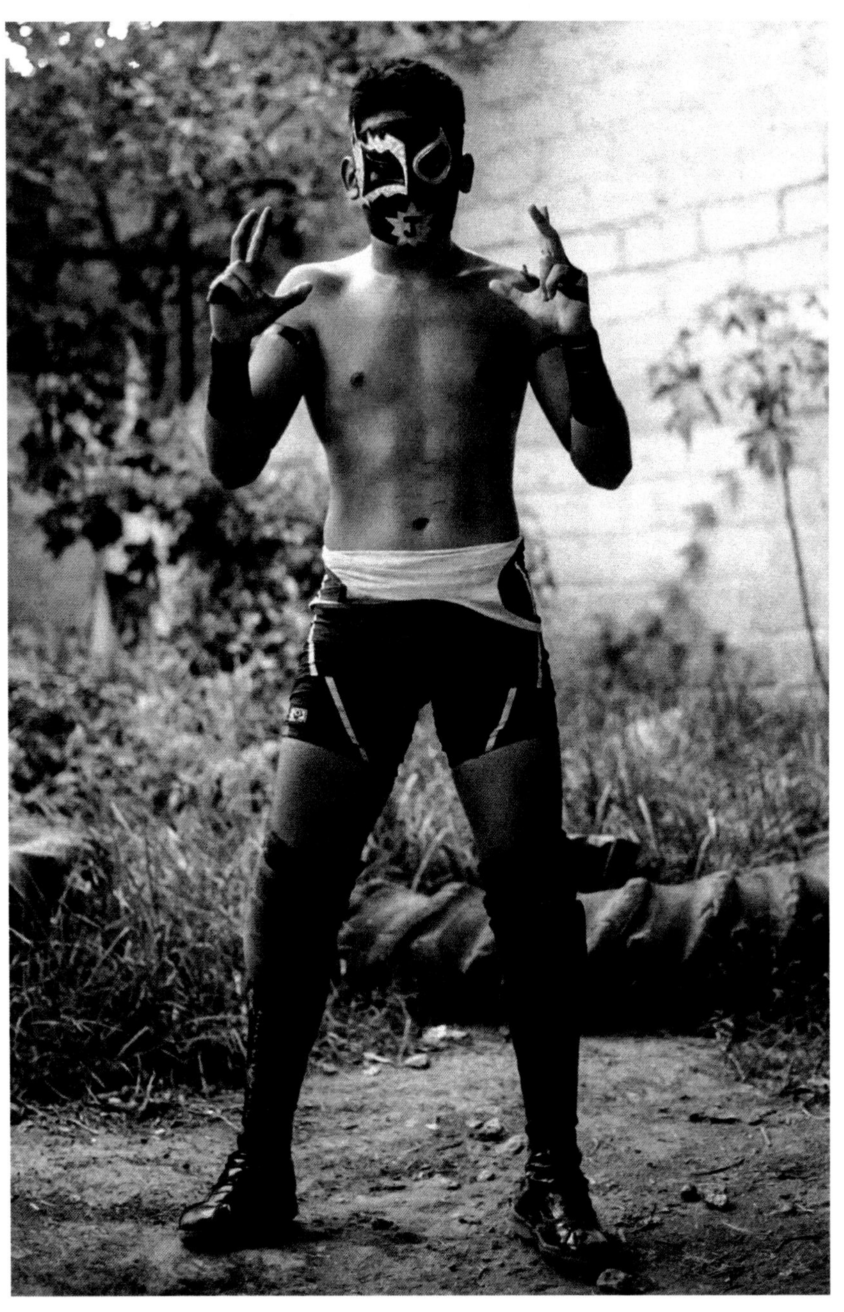

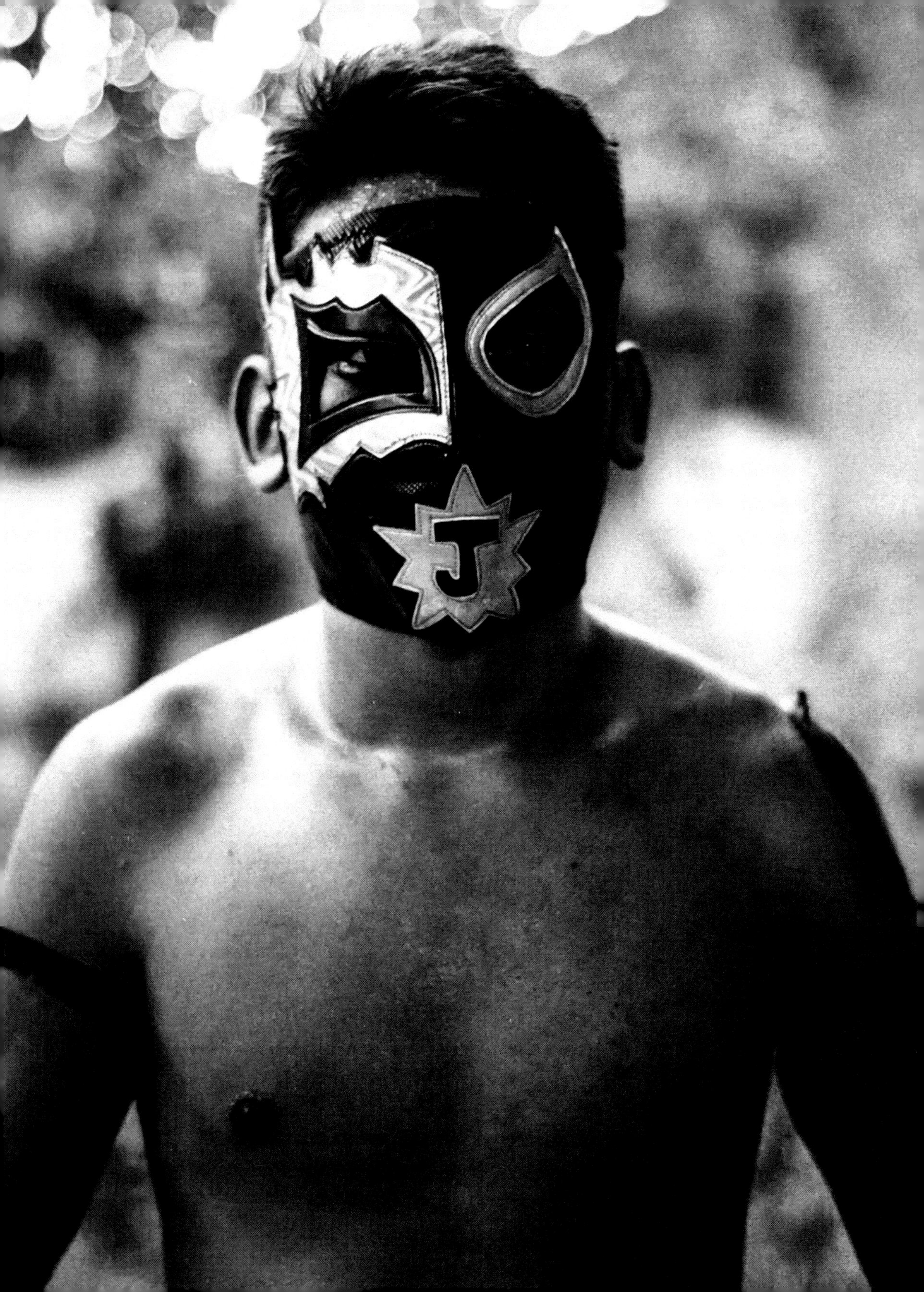
J

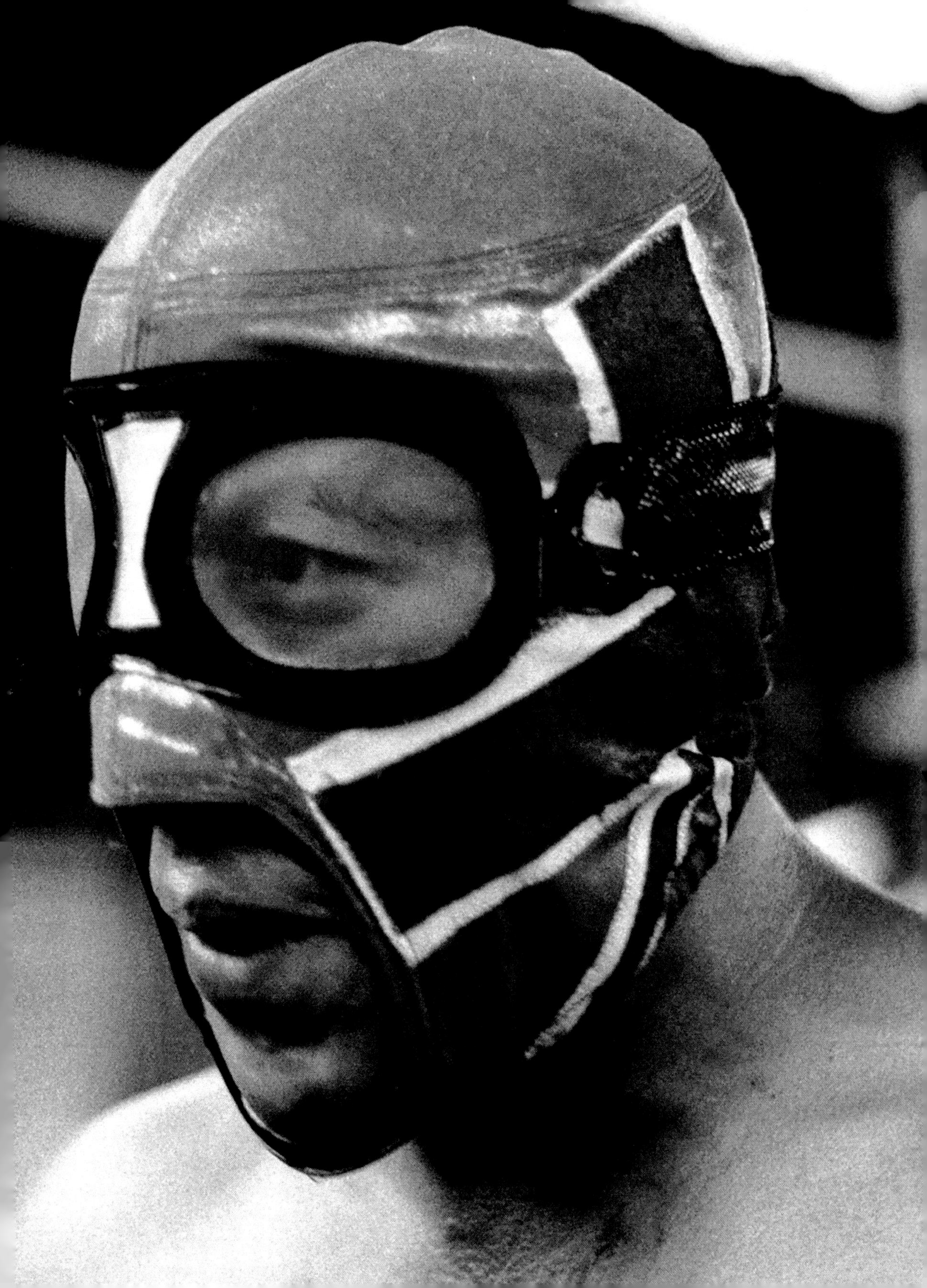

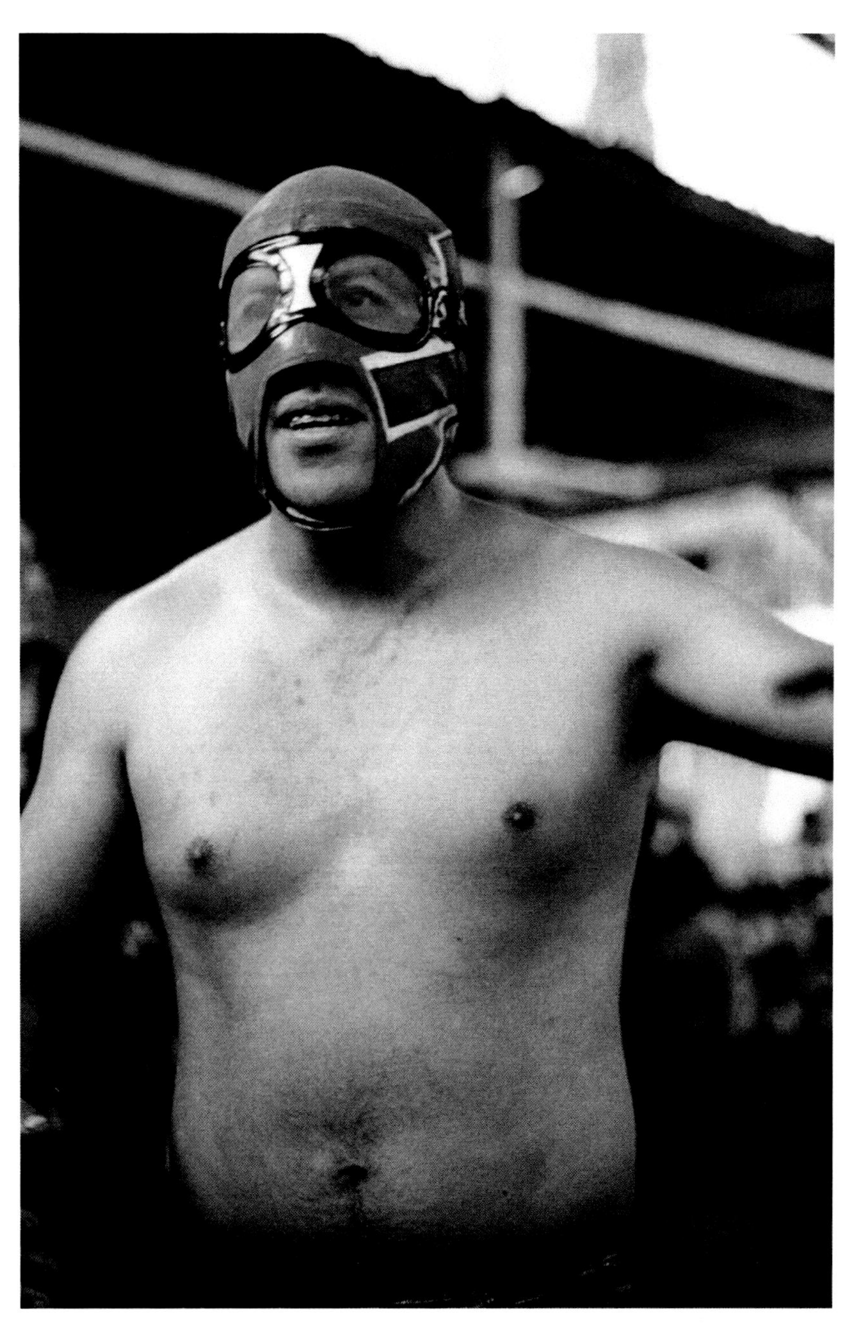

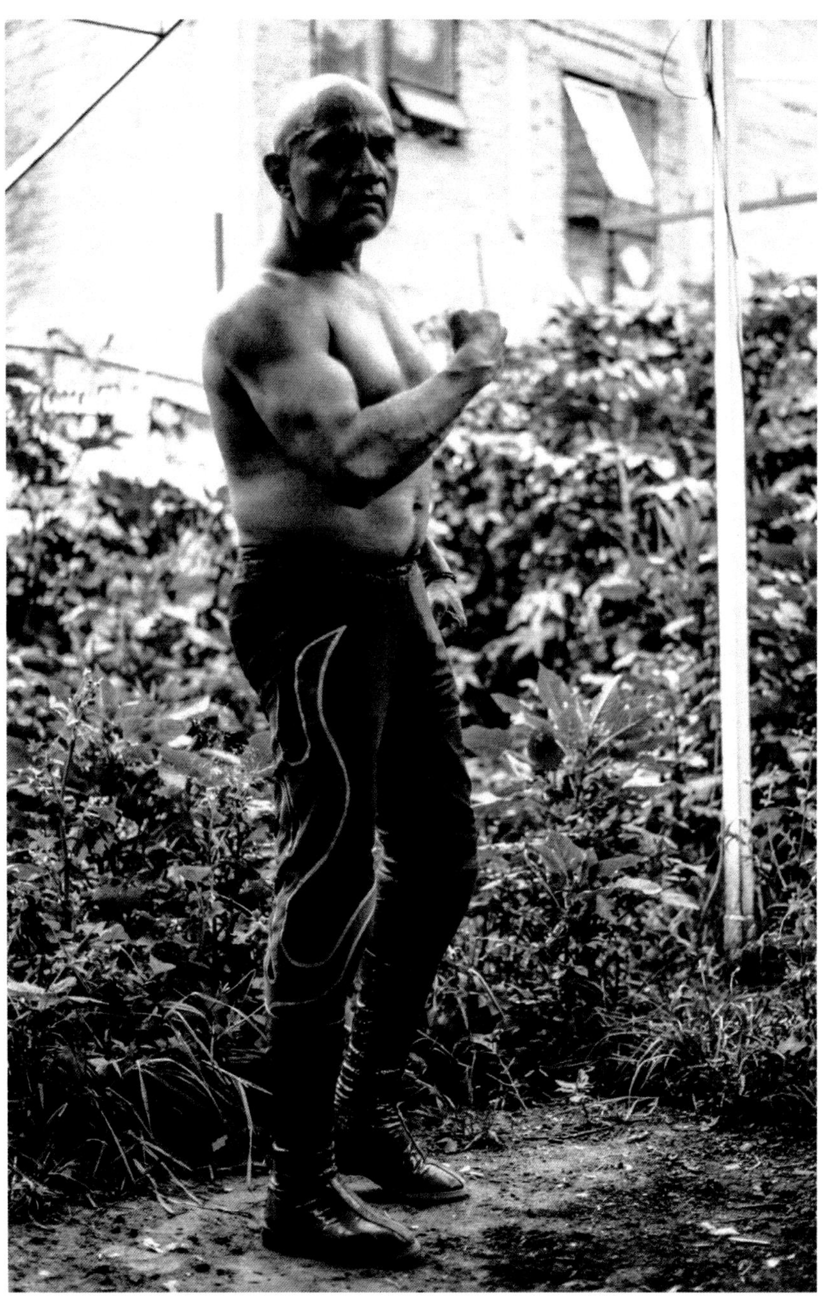

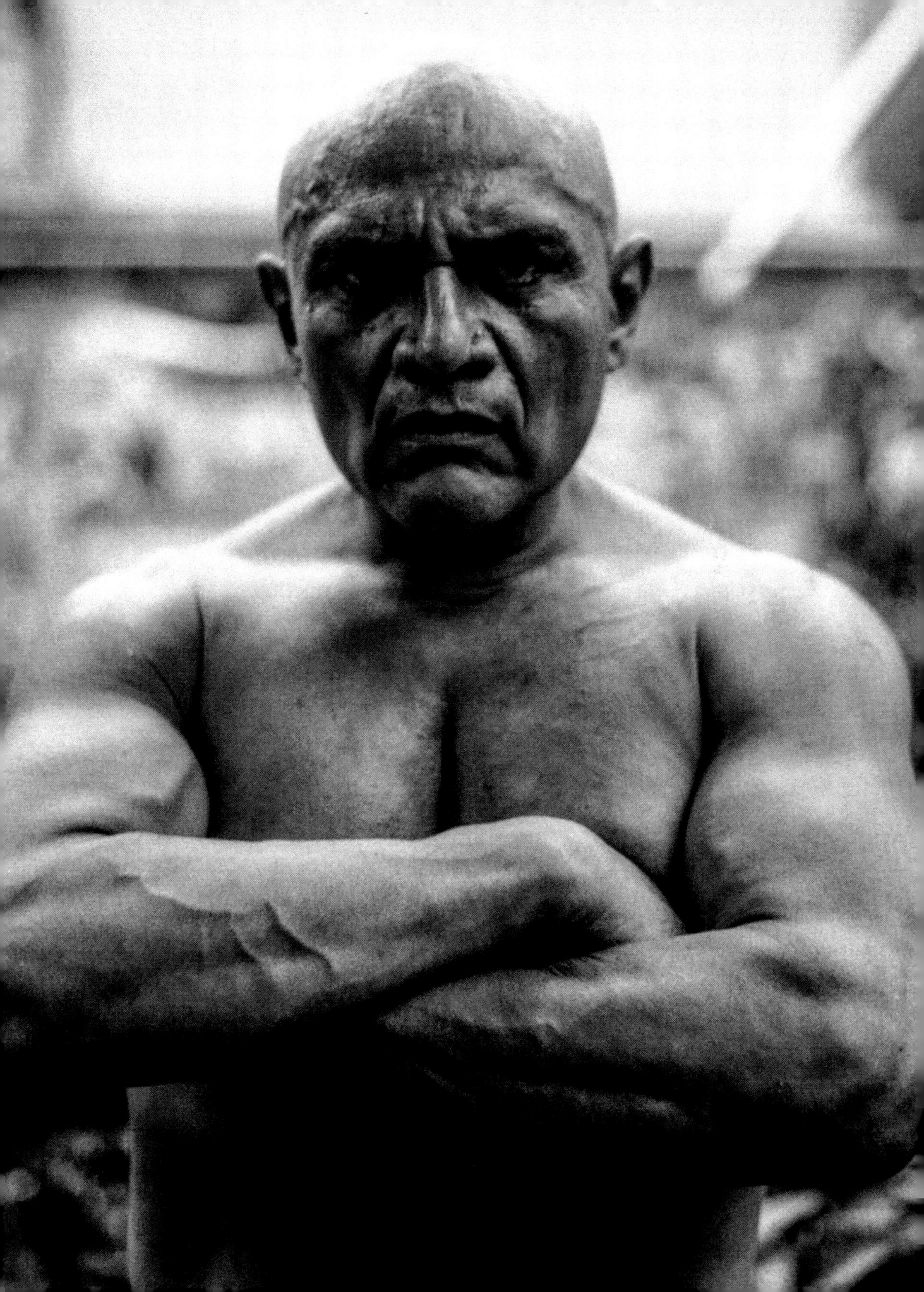

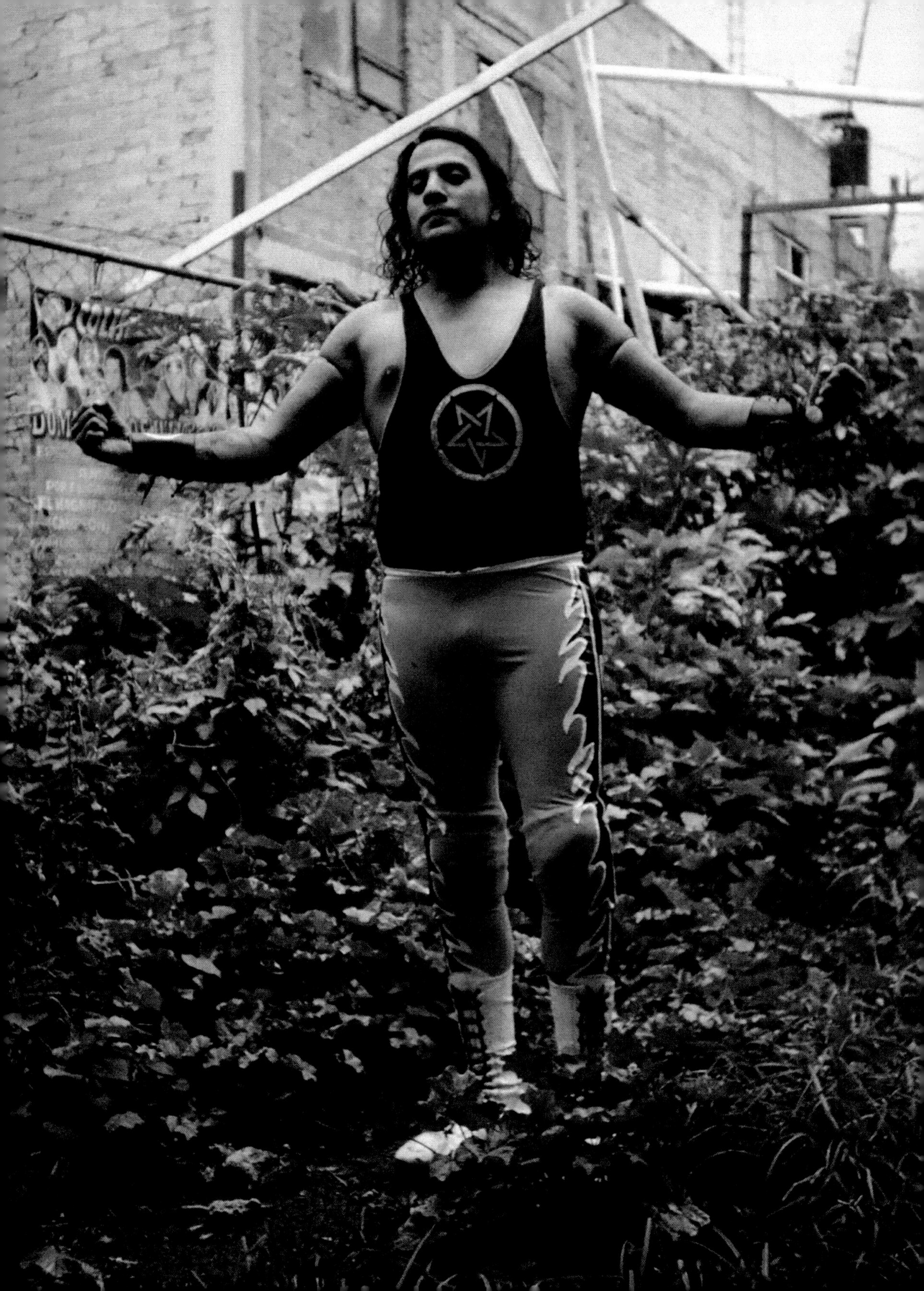

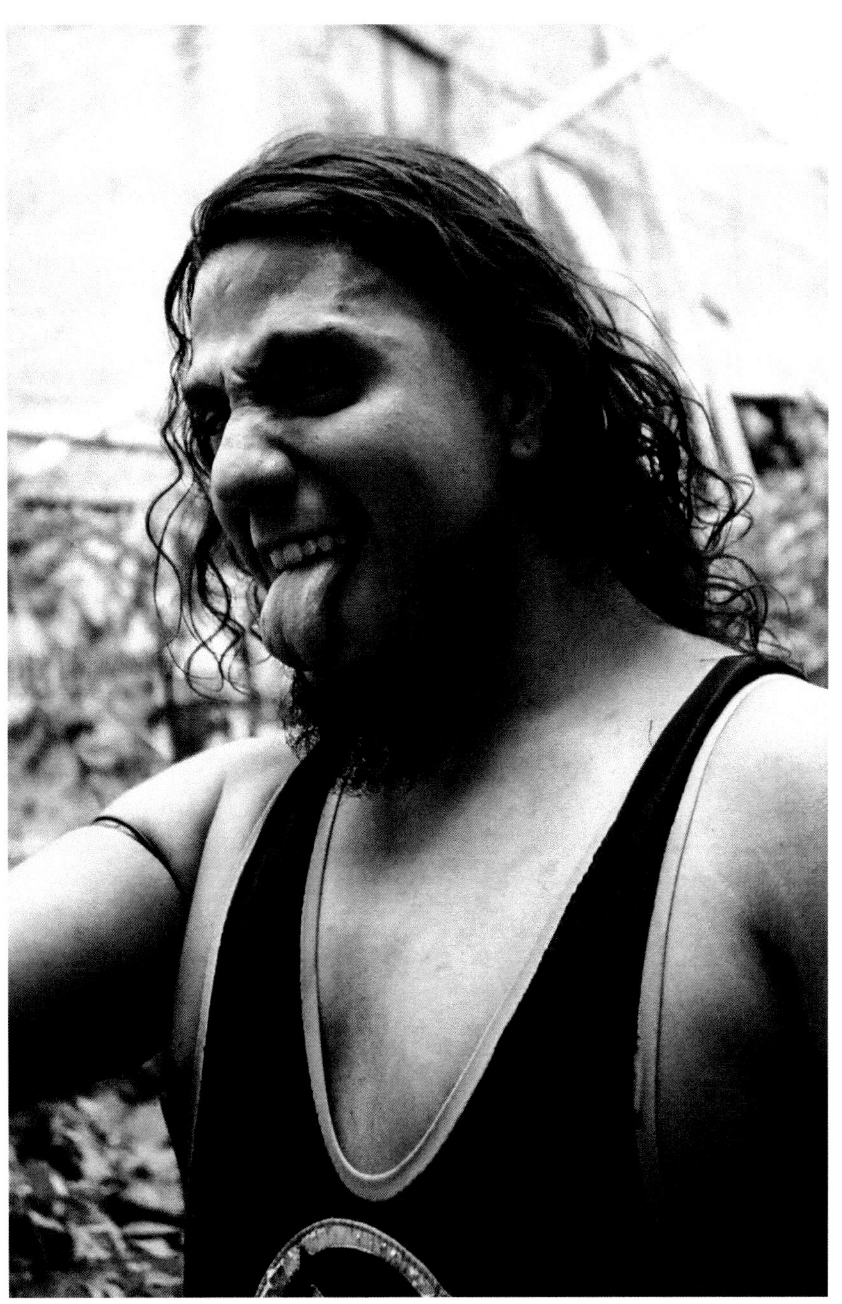

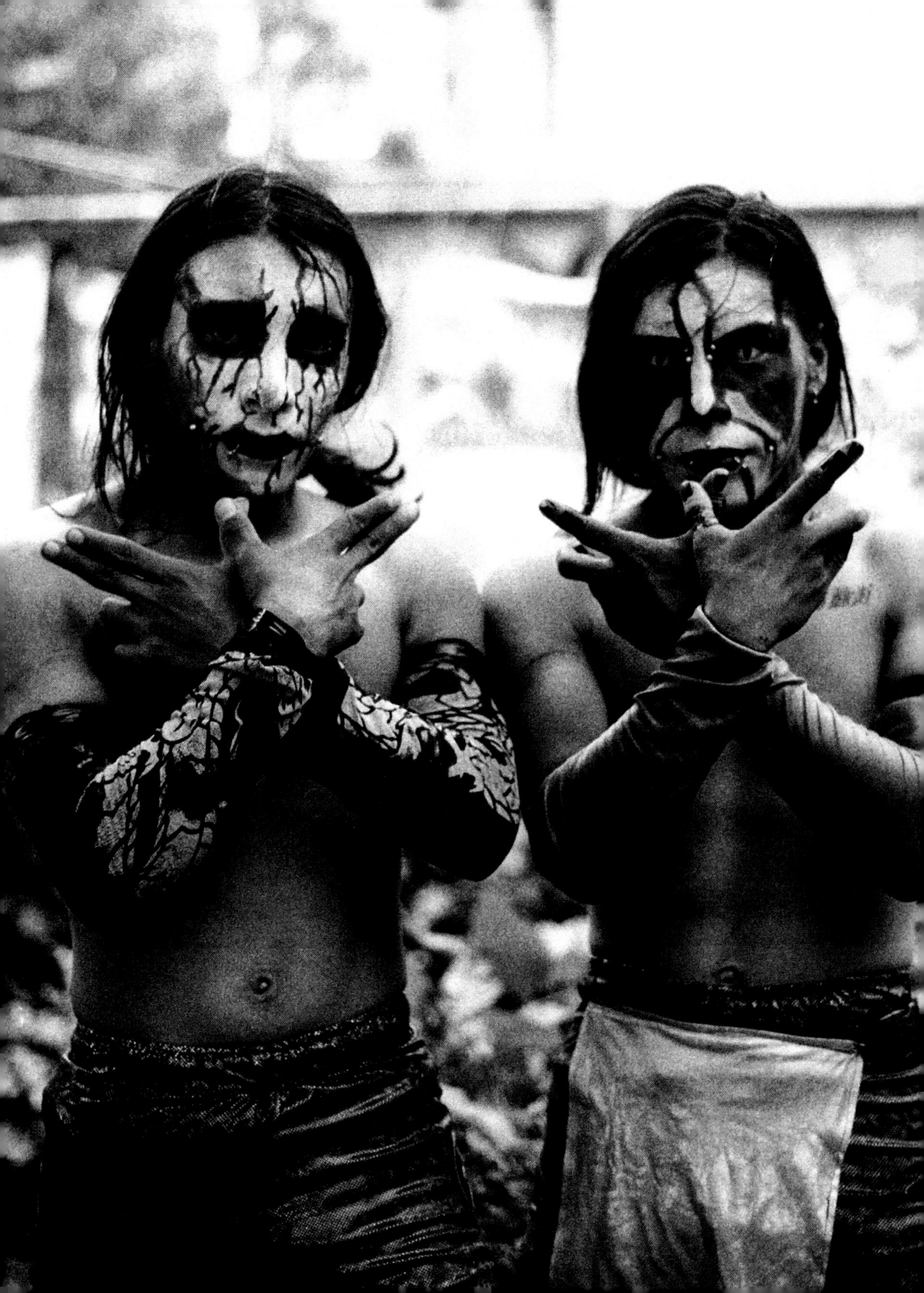

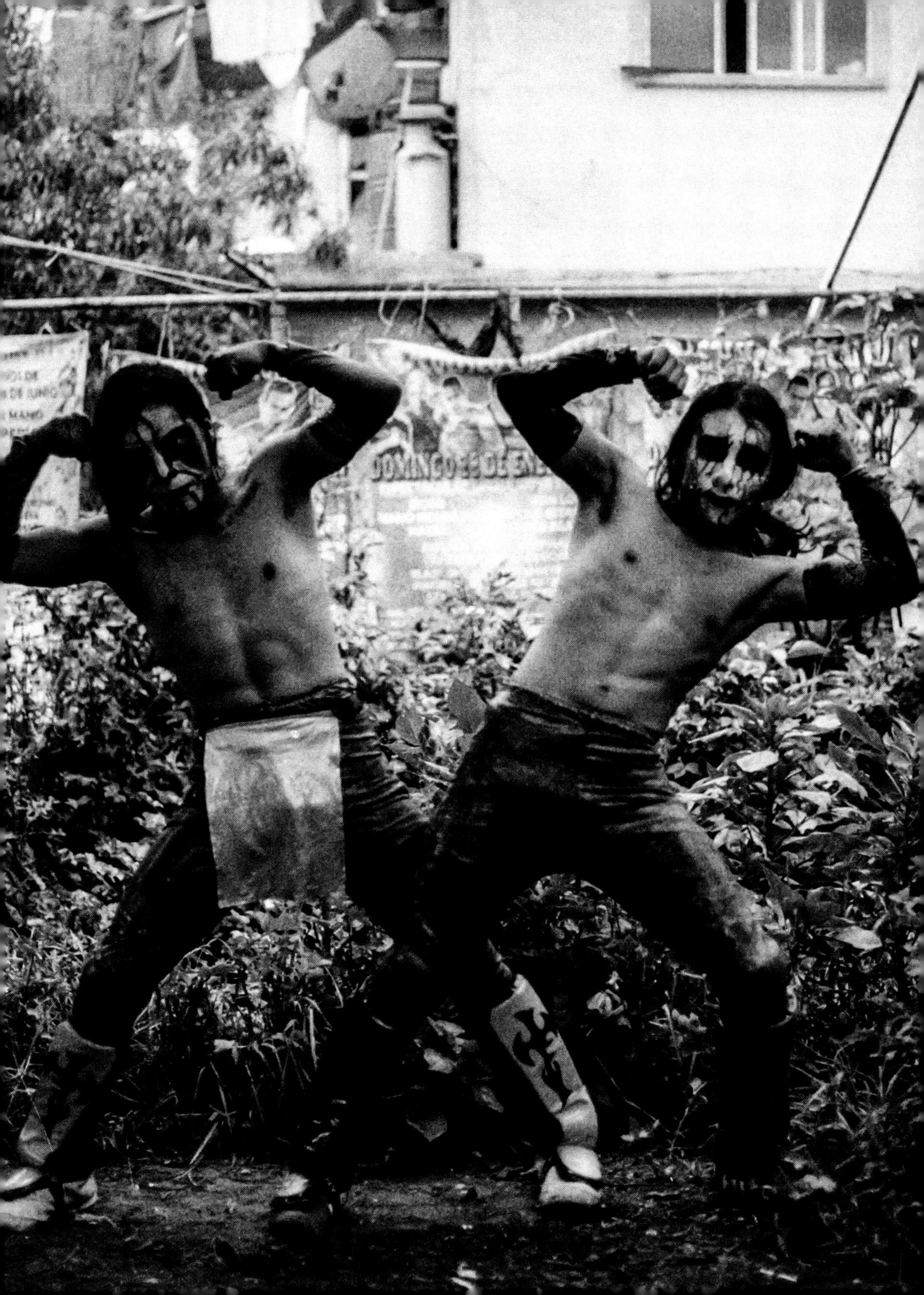

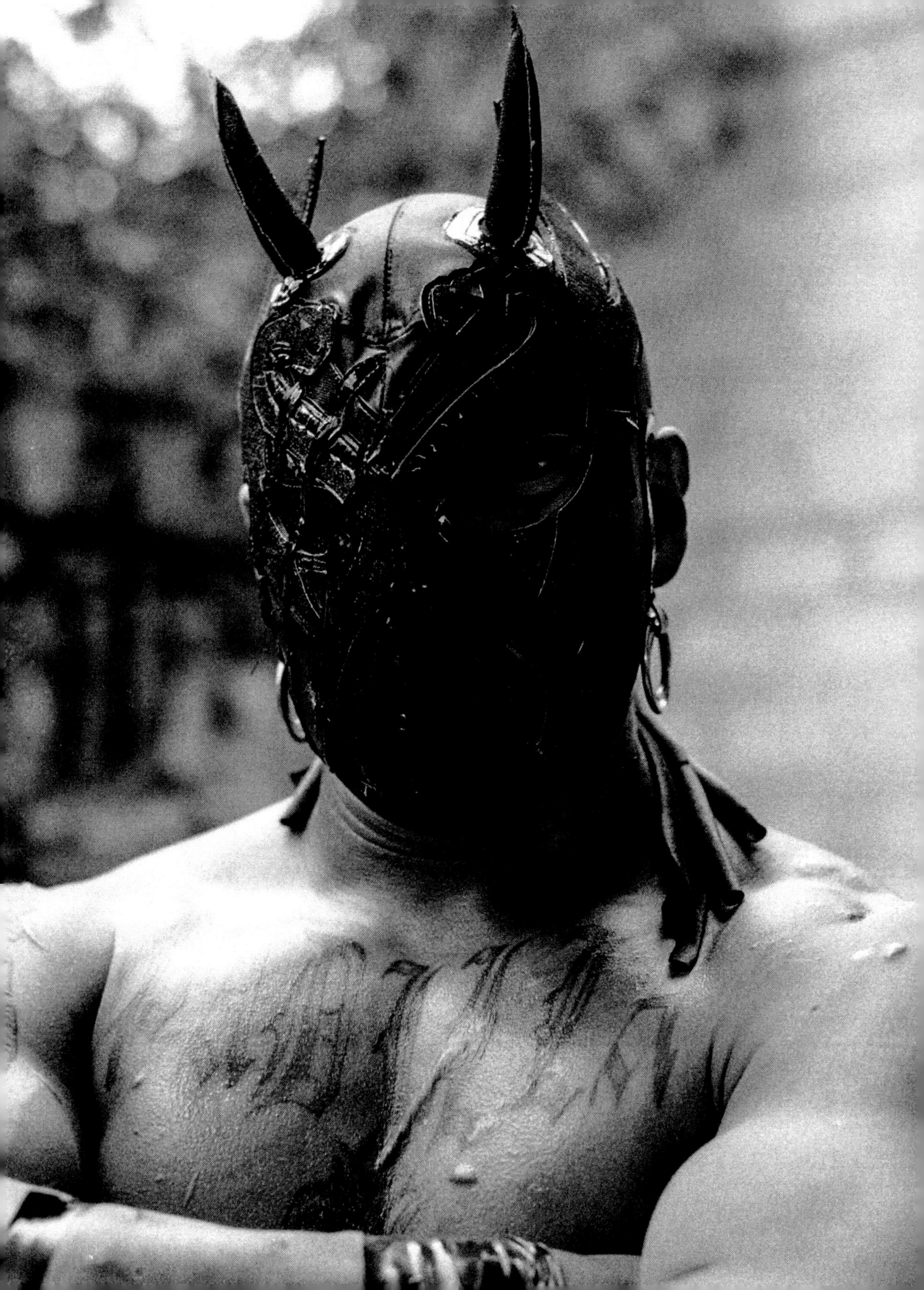

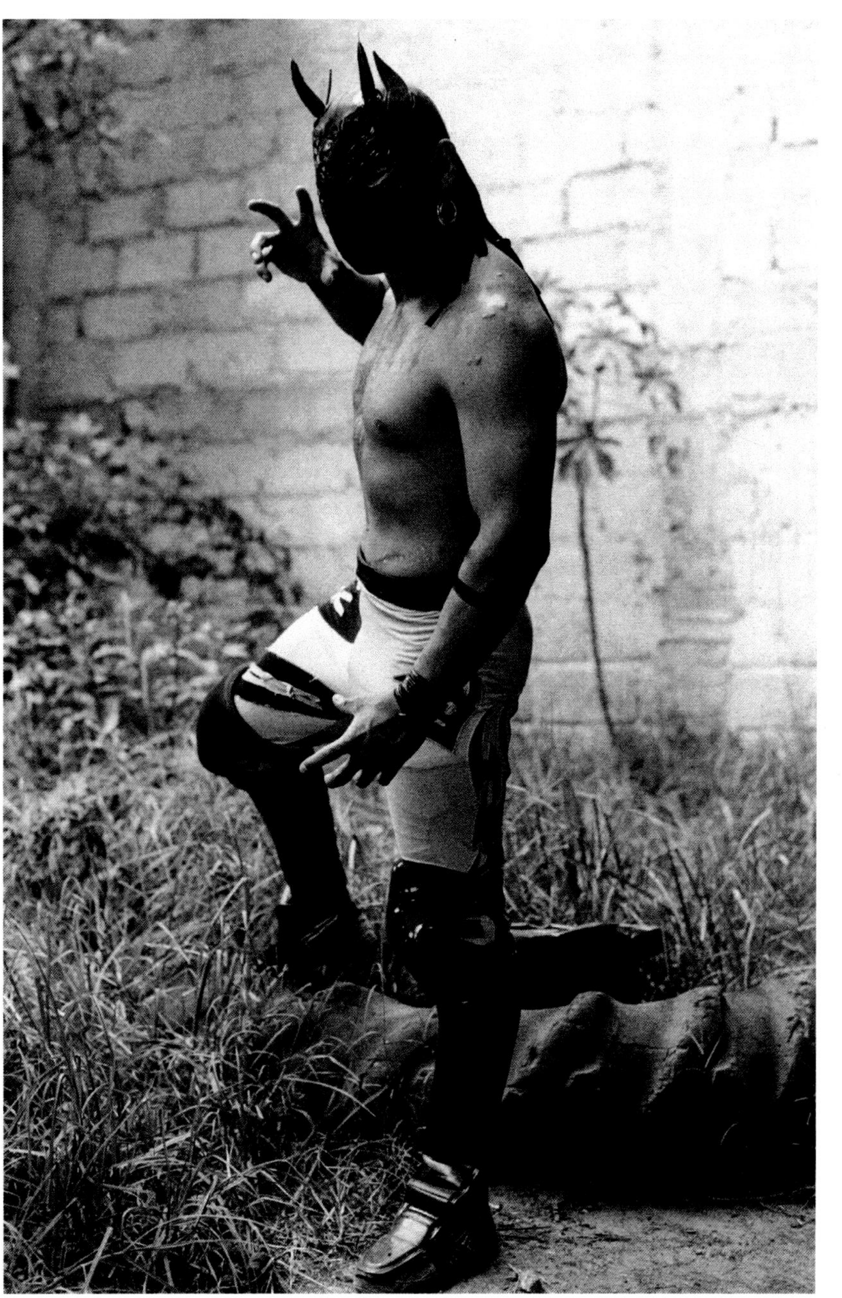

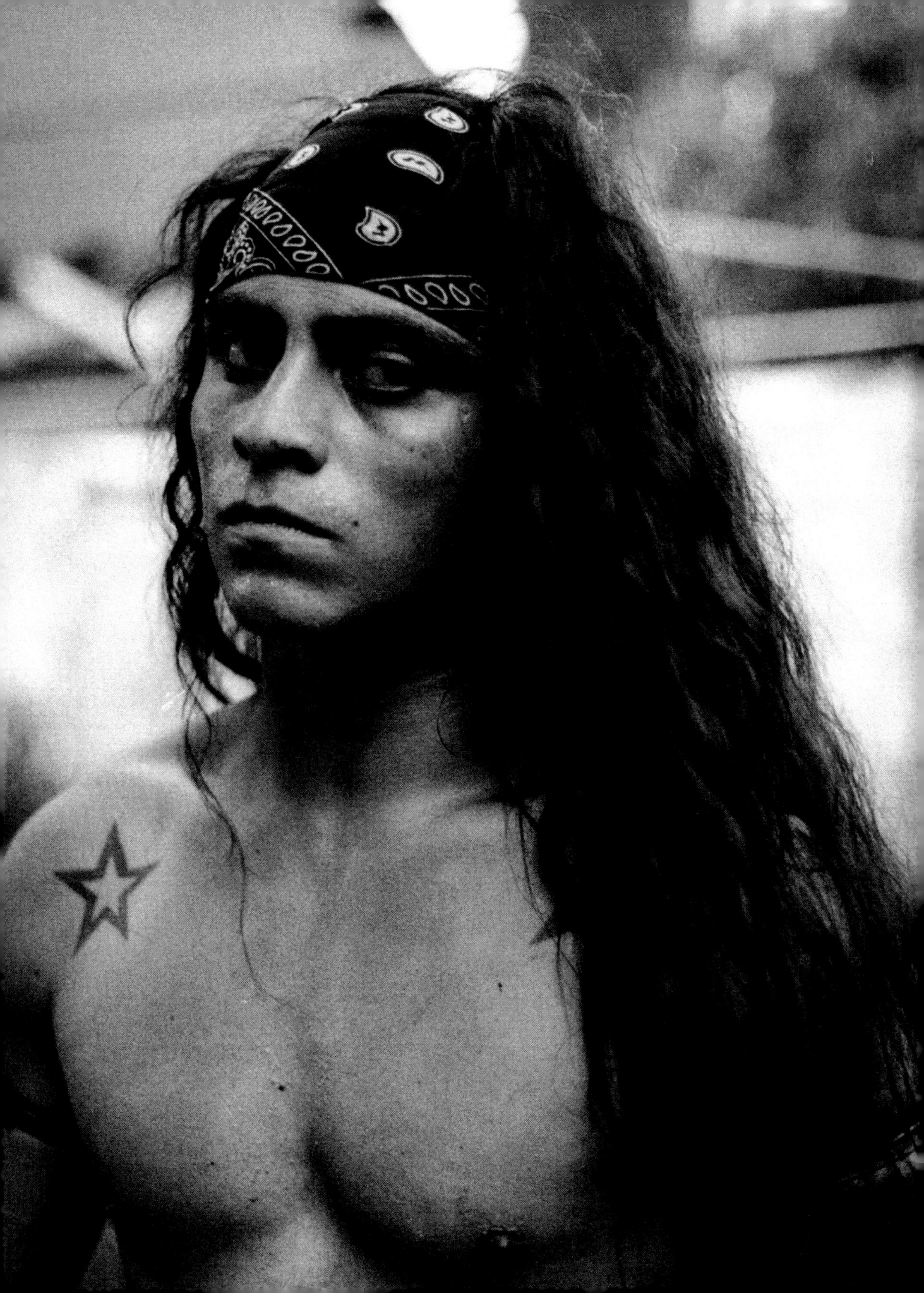

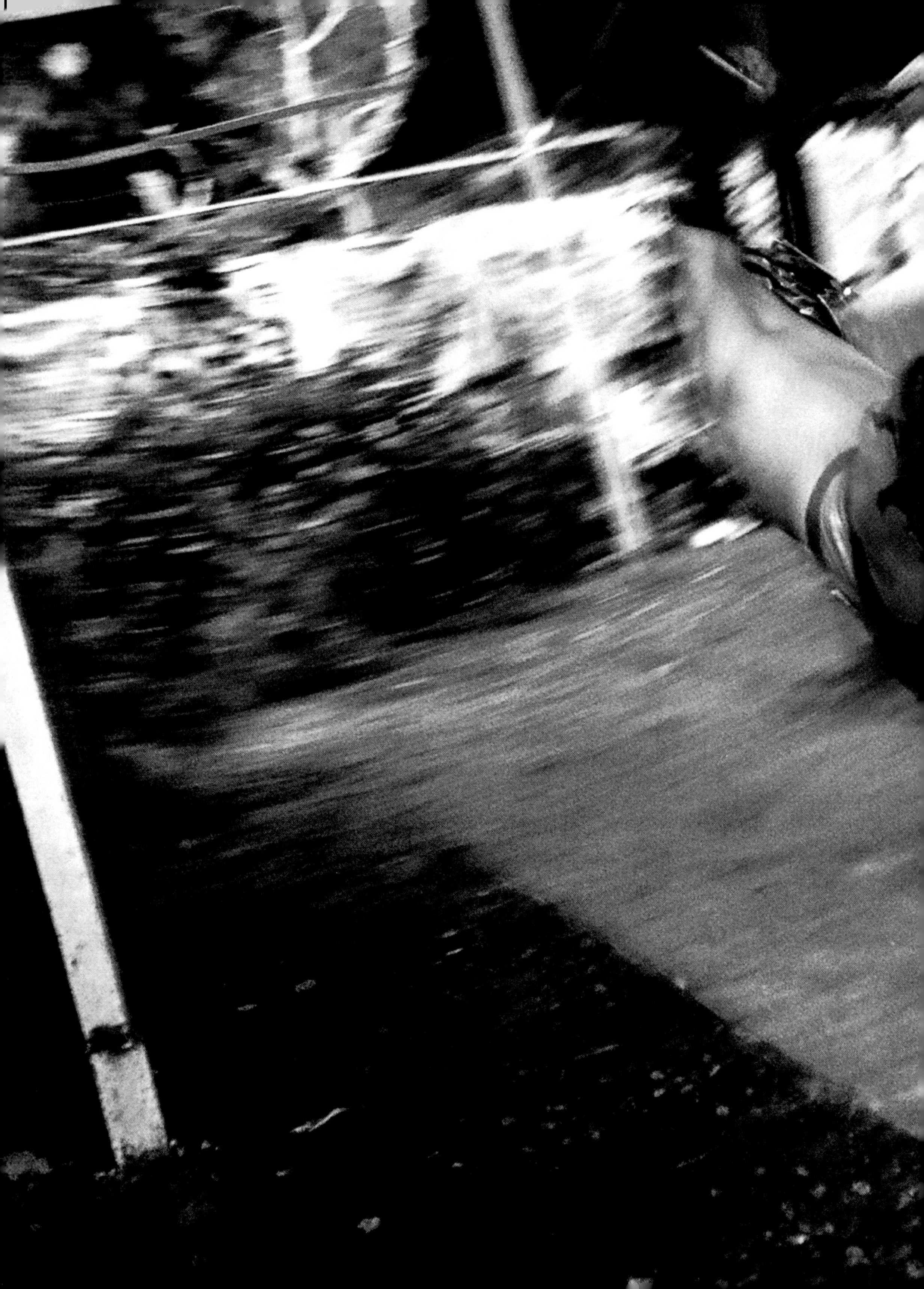

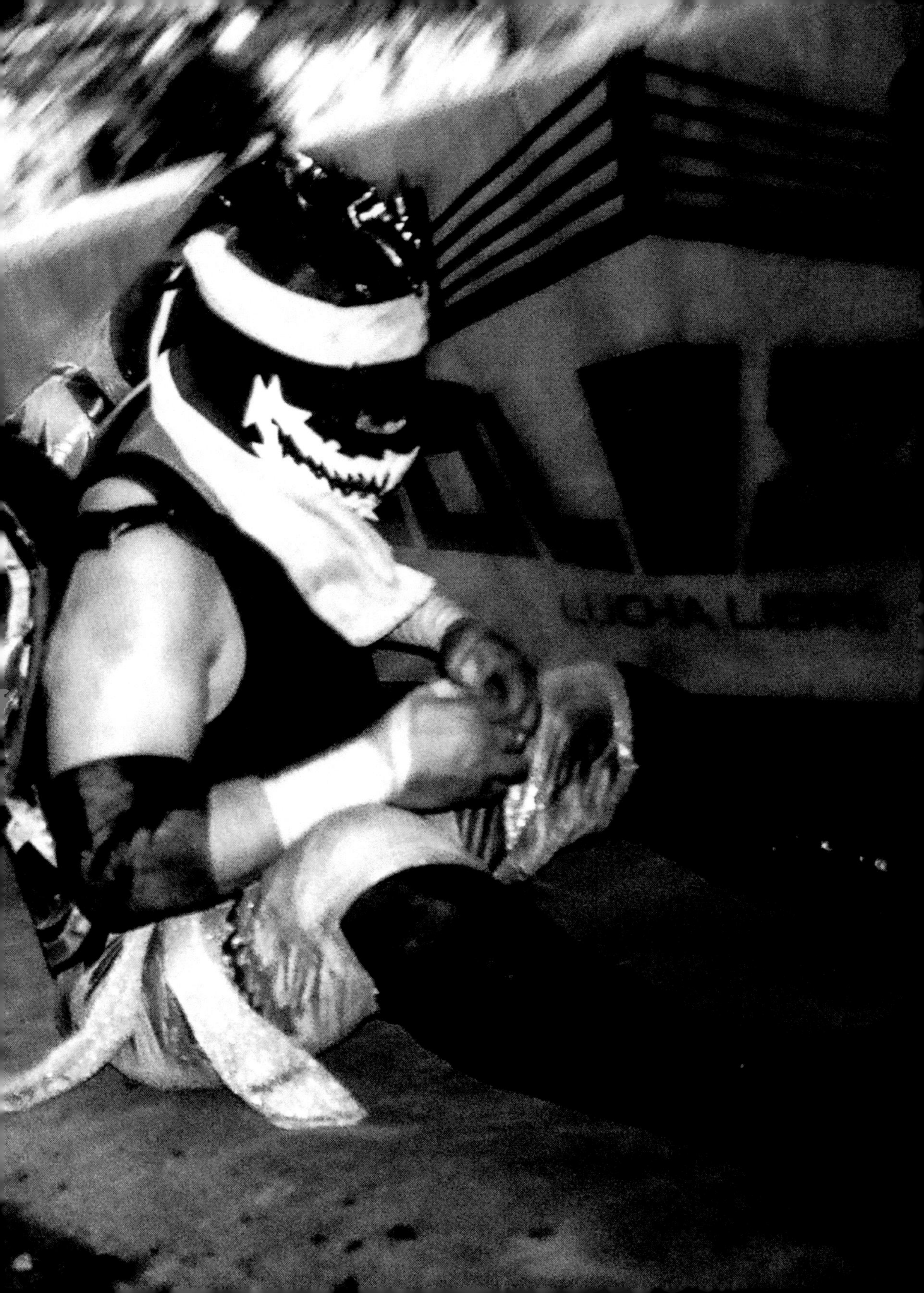

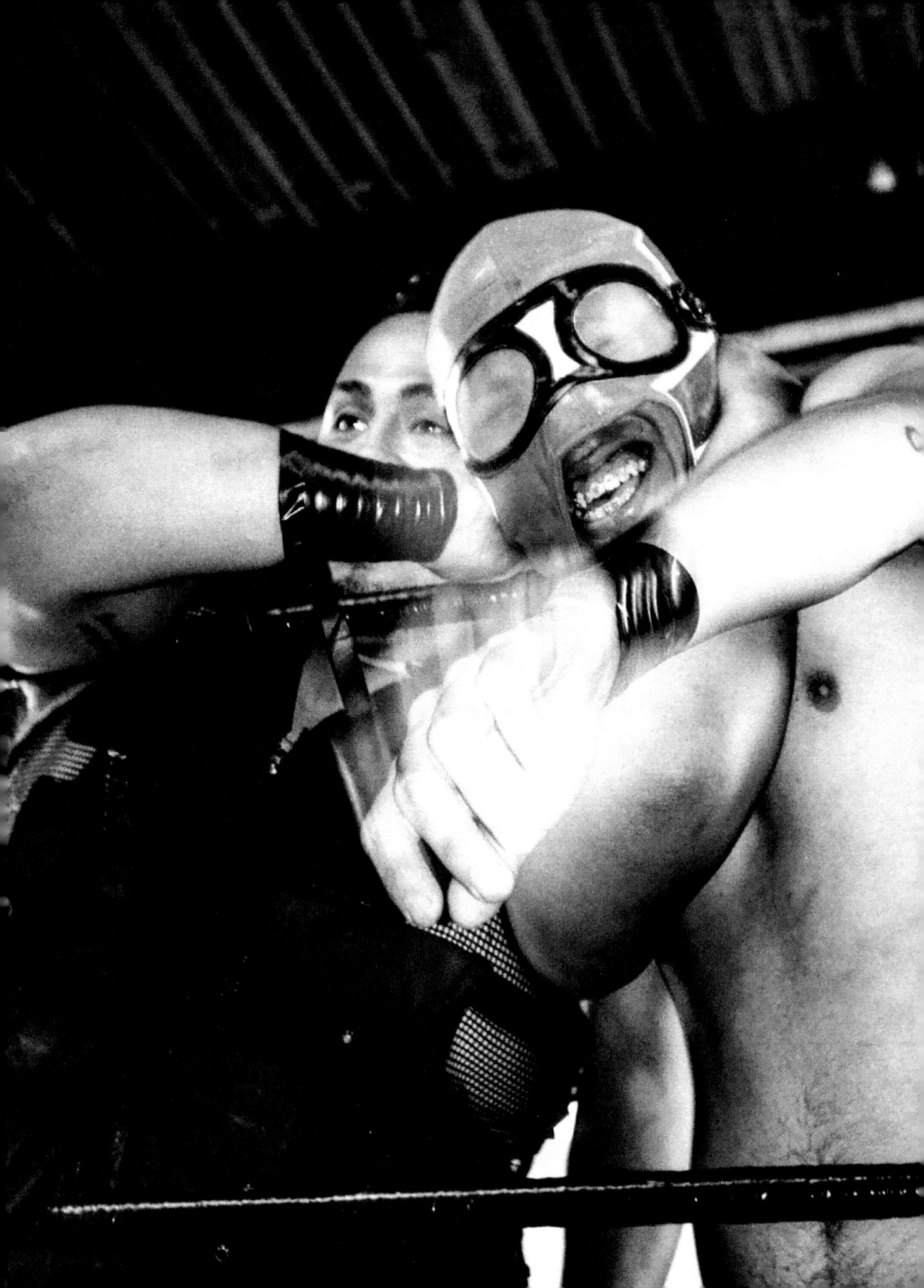

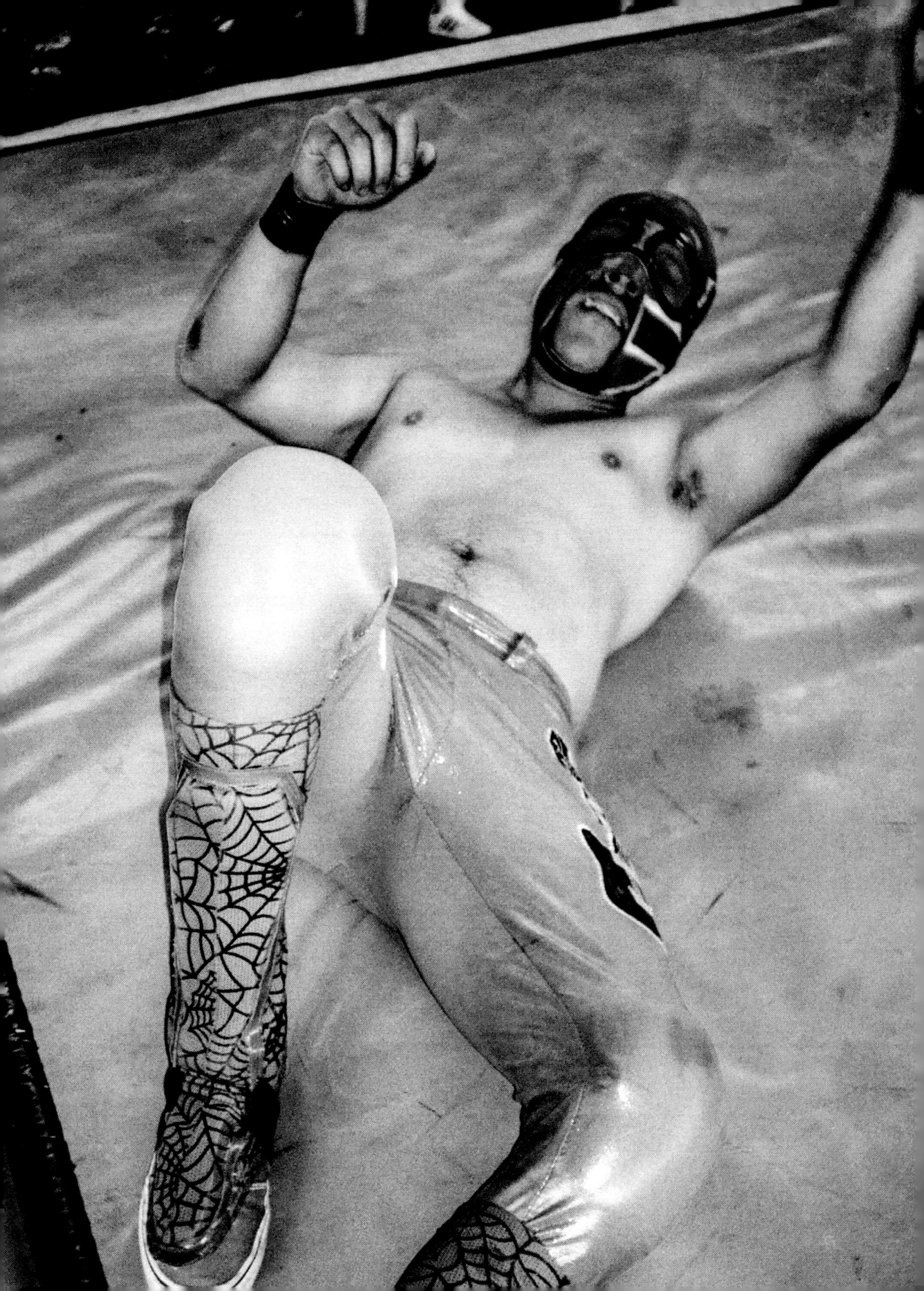

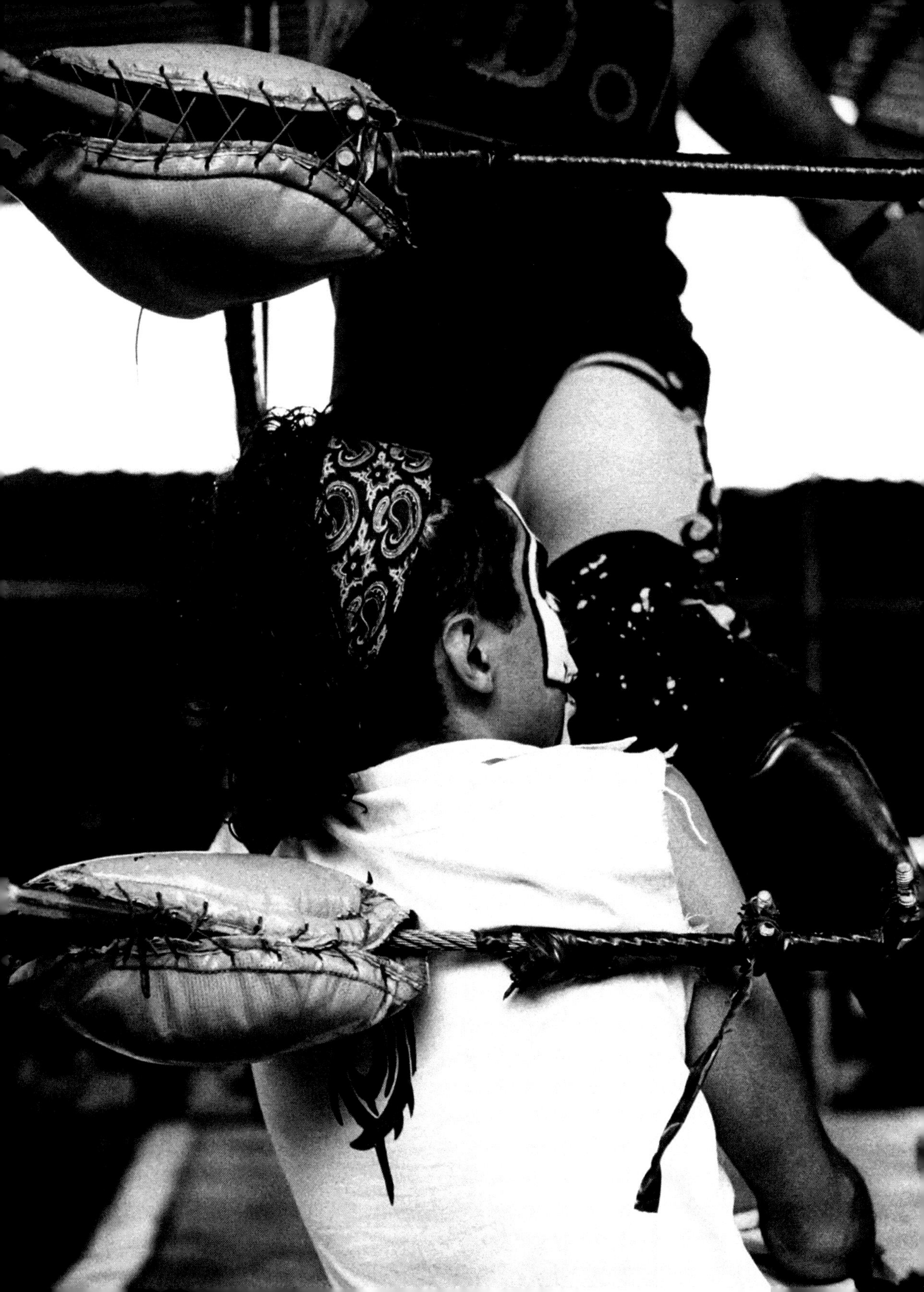

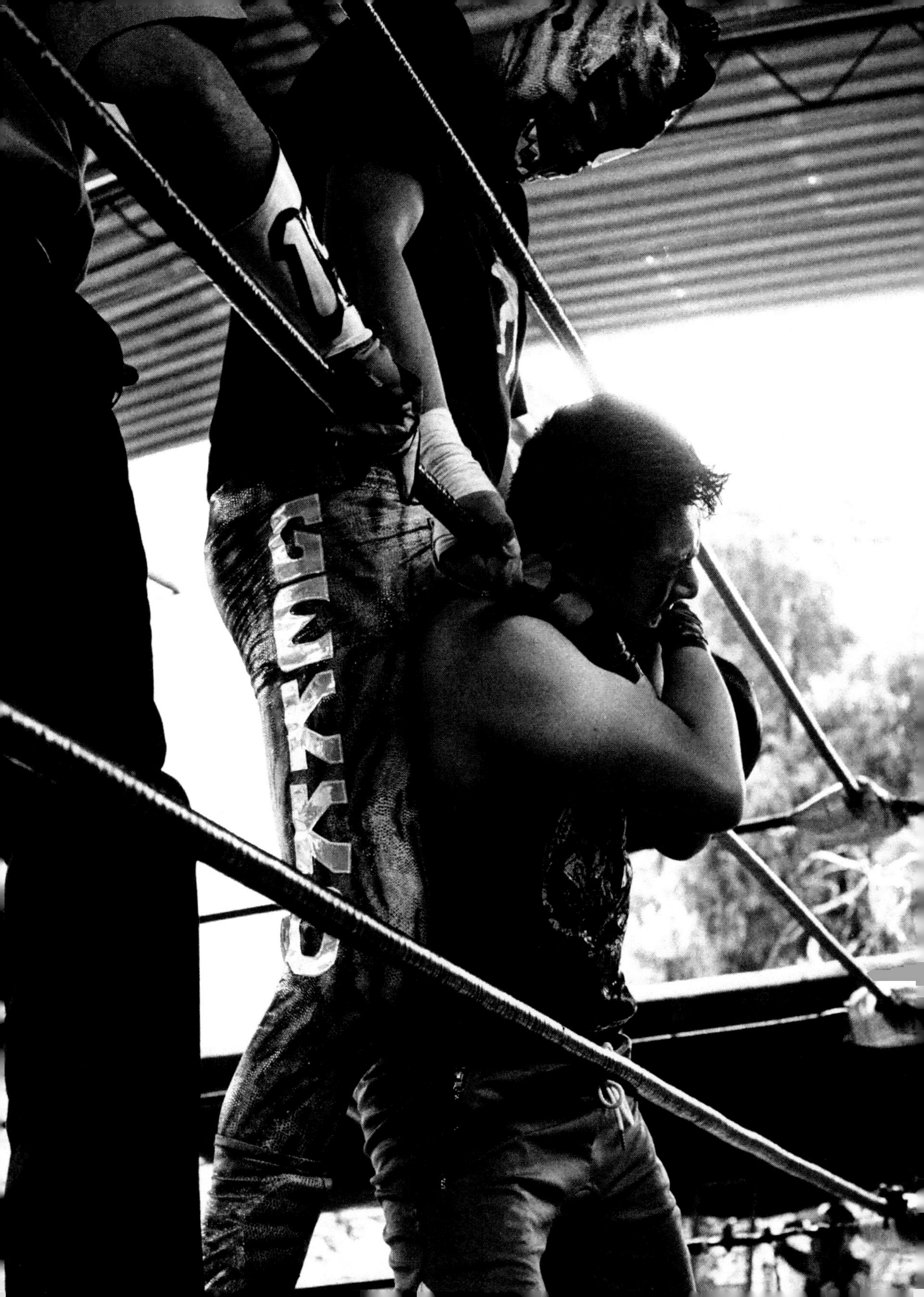

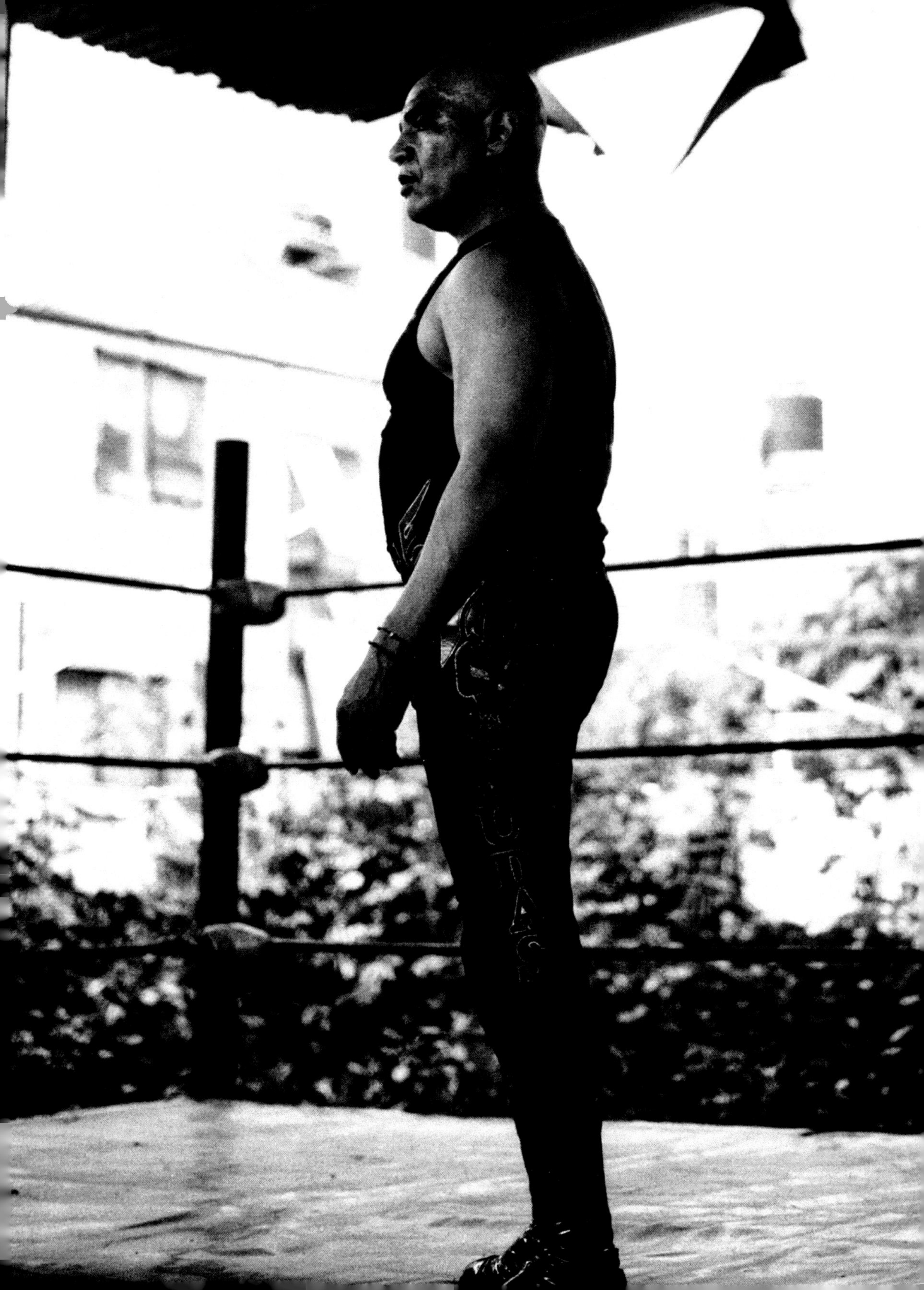

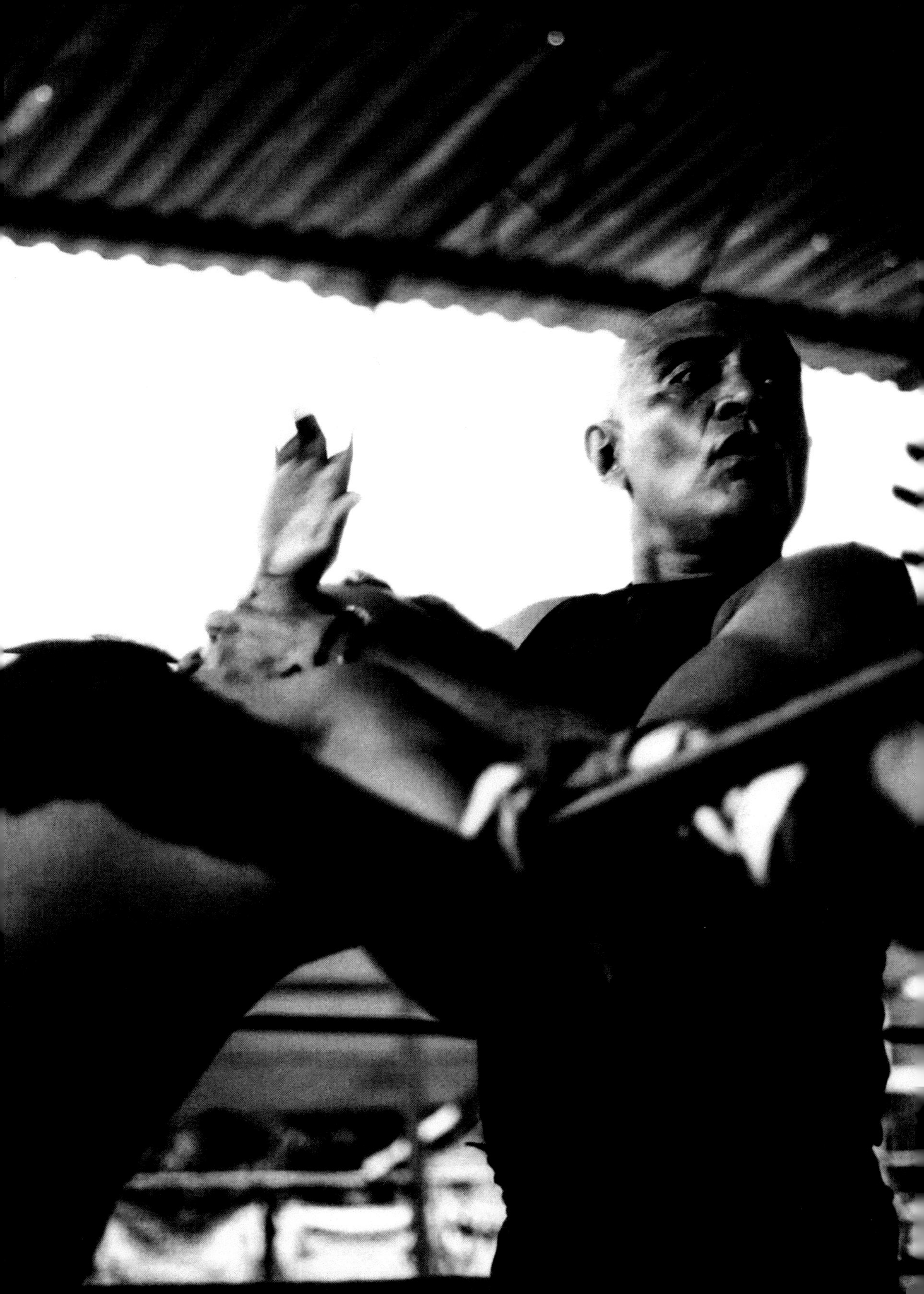

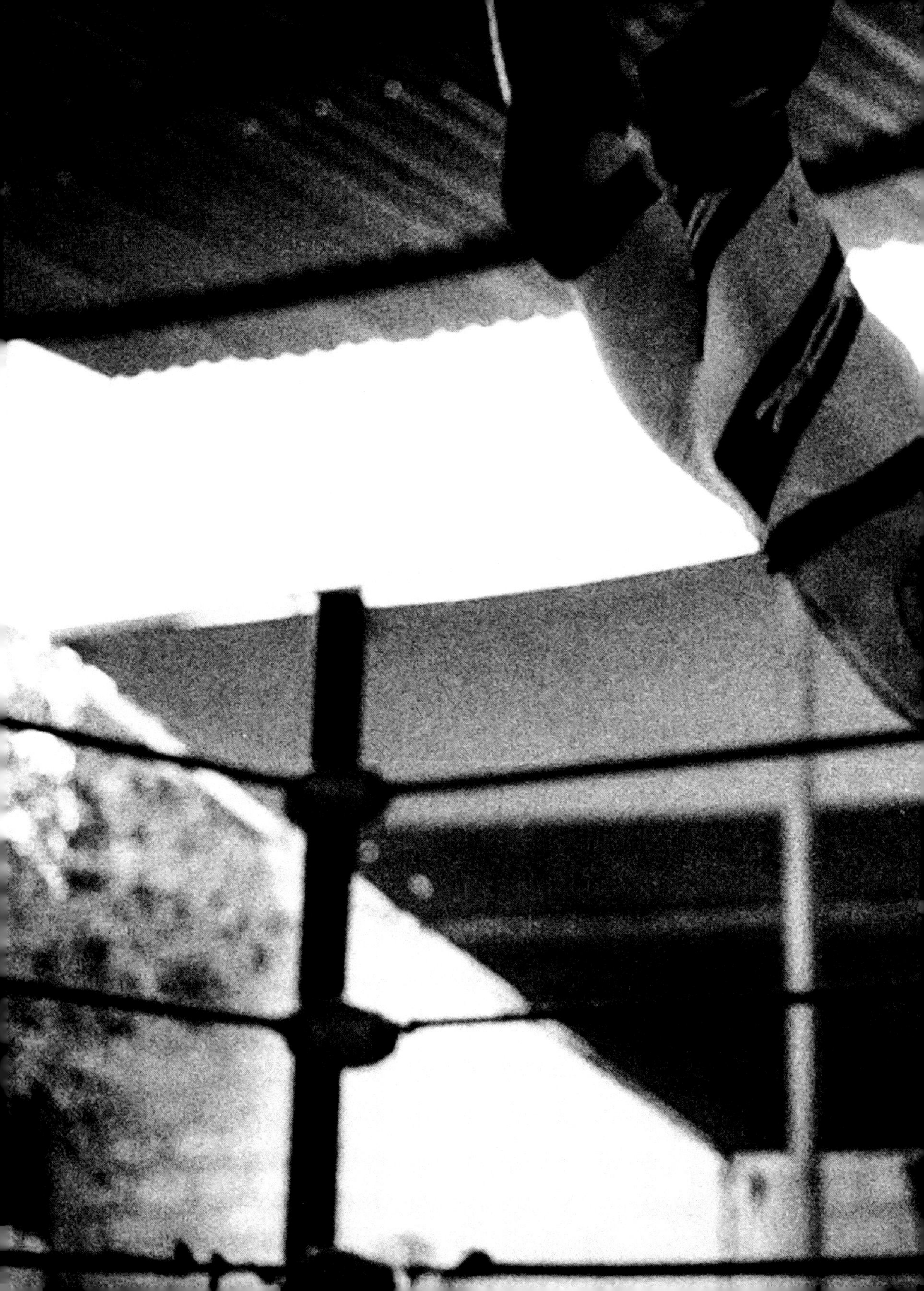

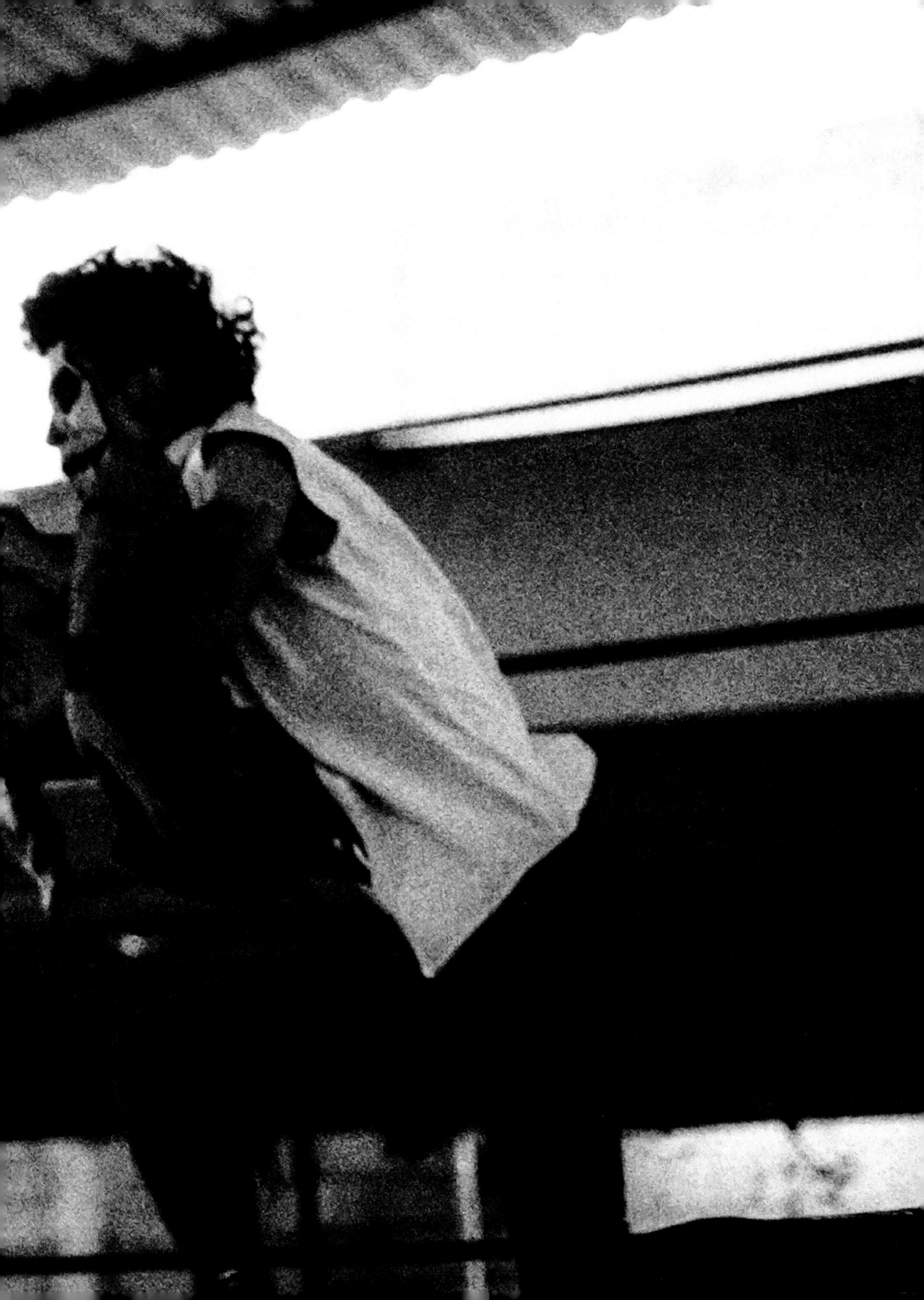

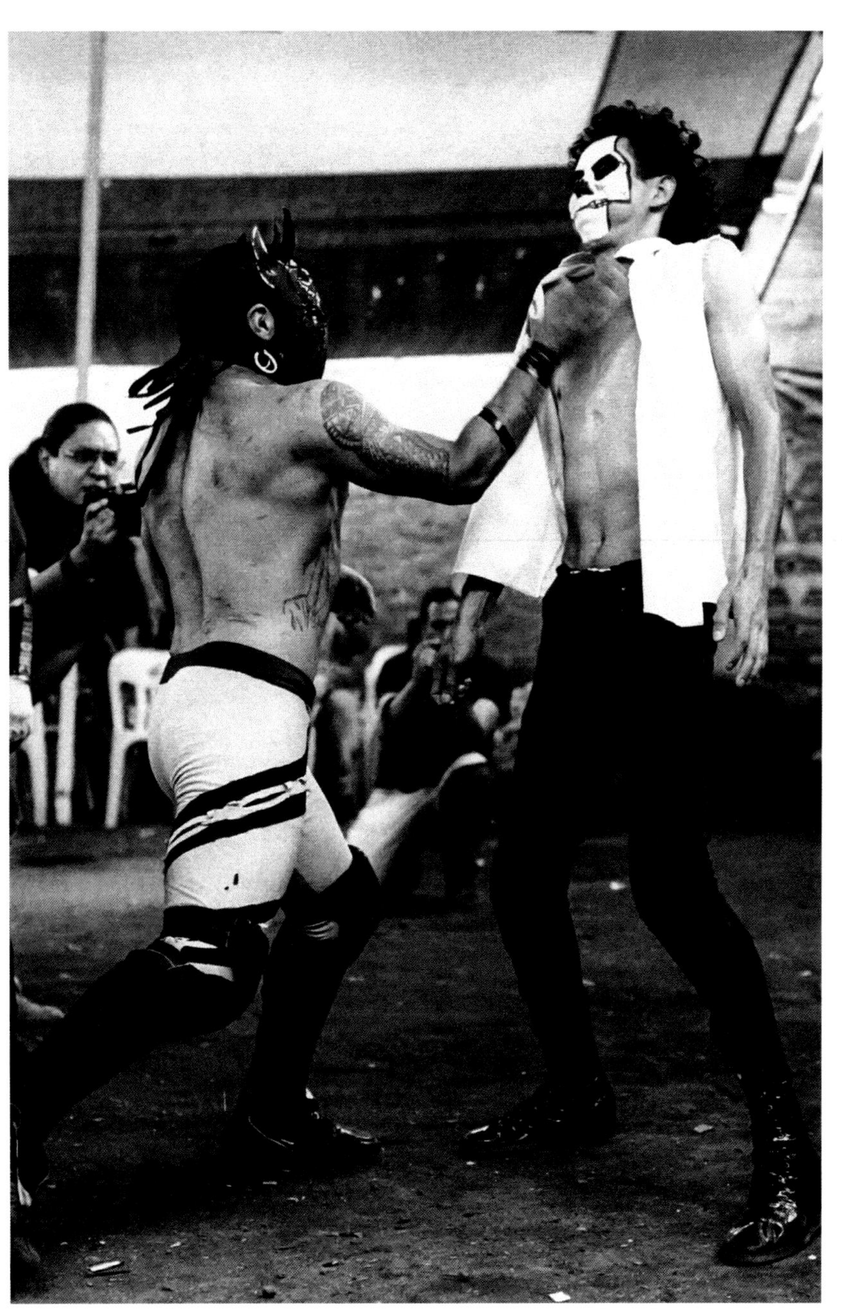

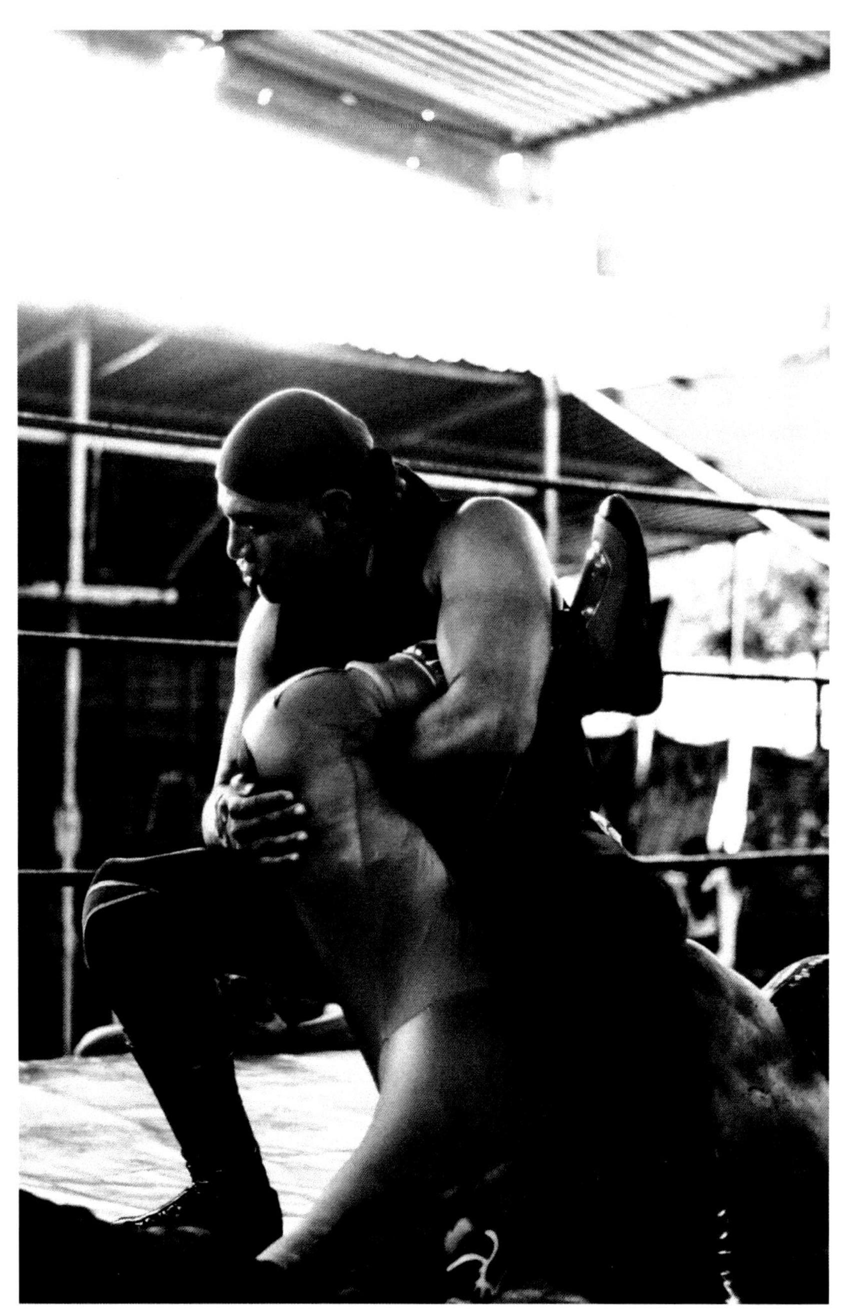

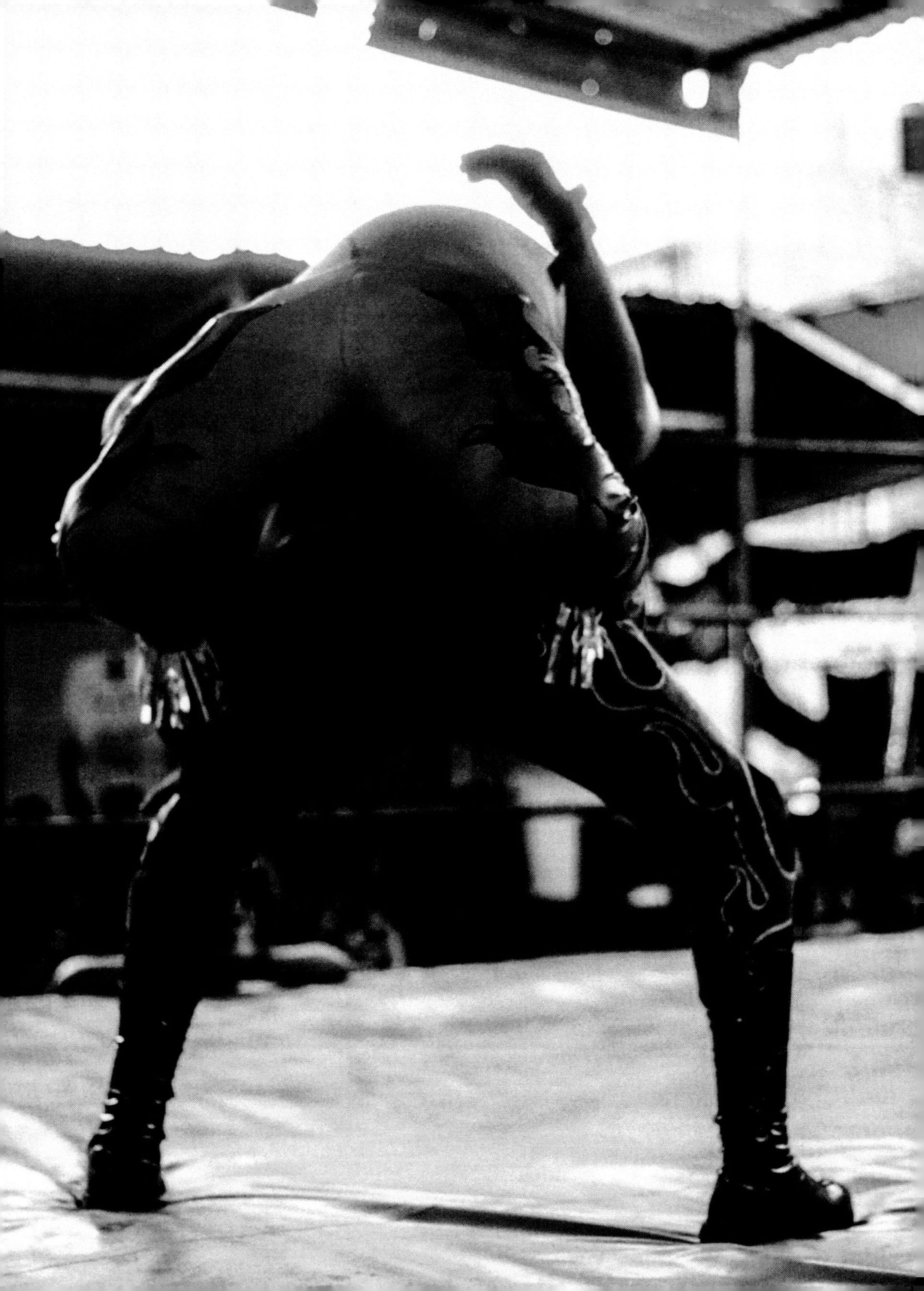

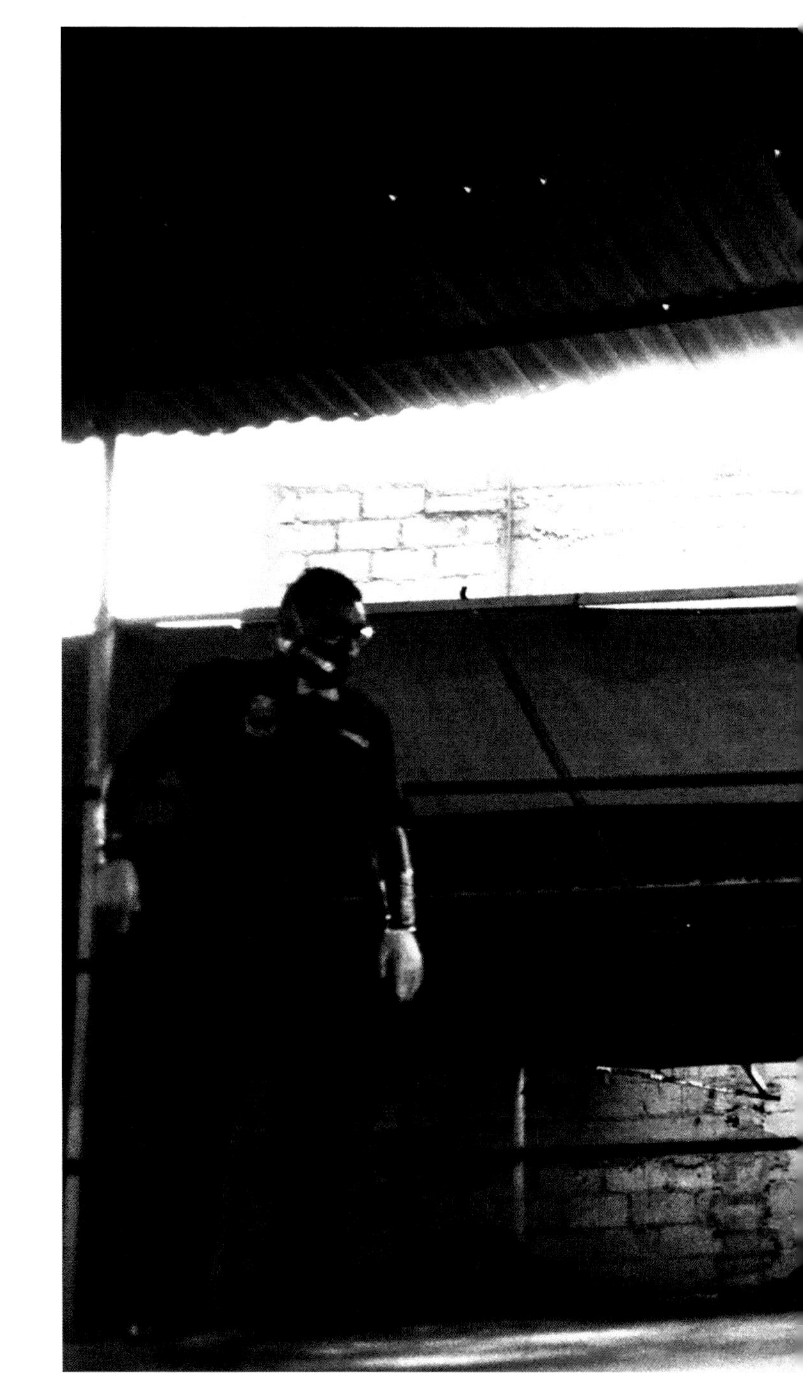

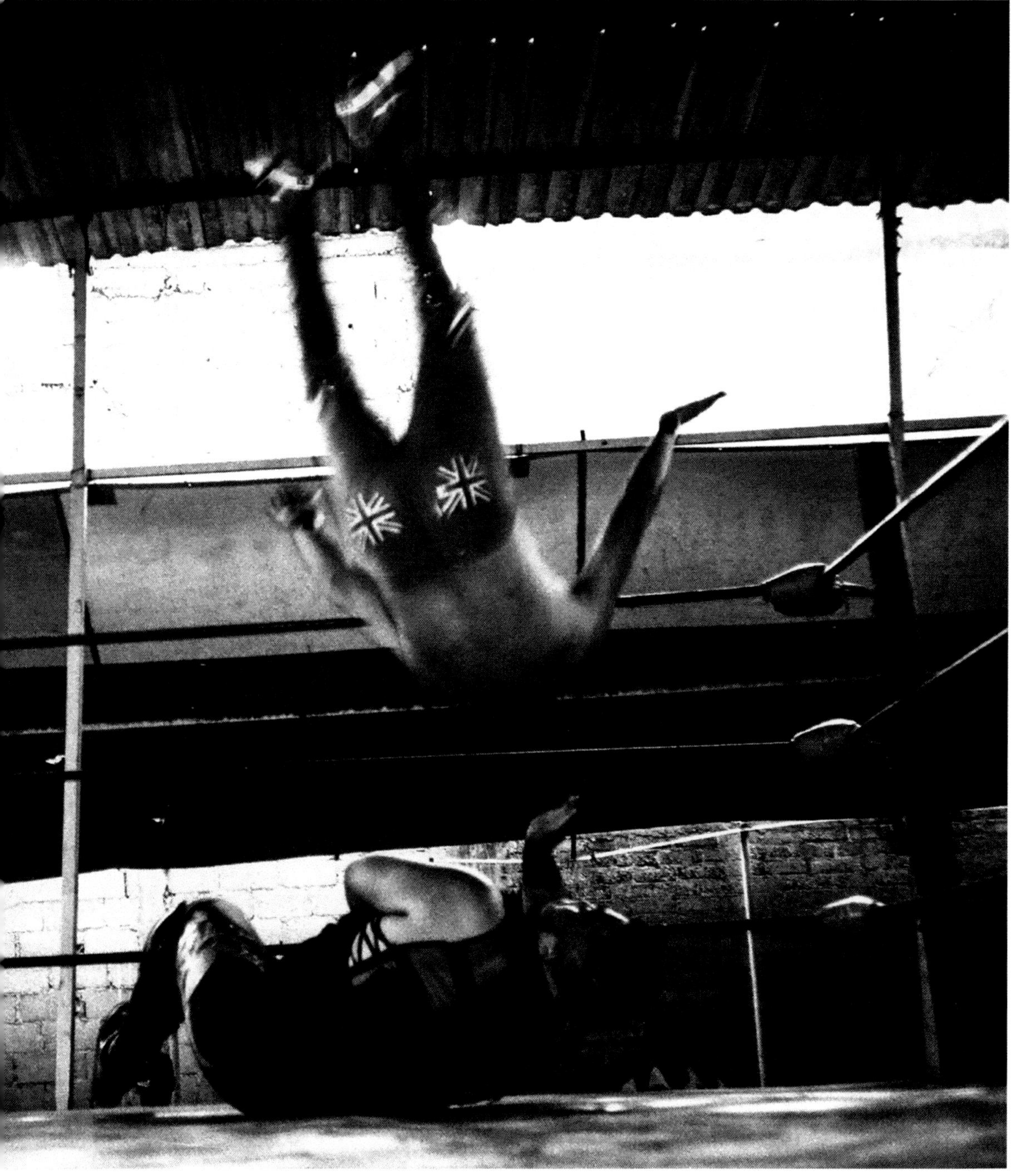

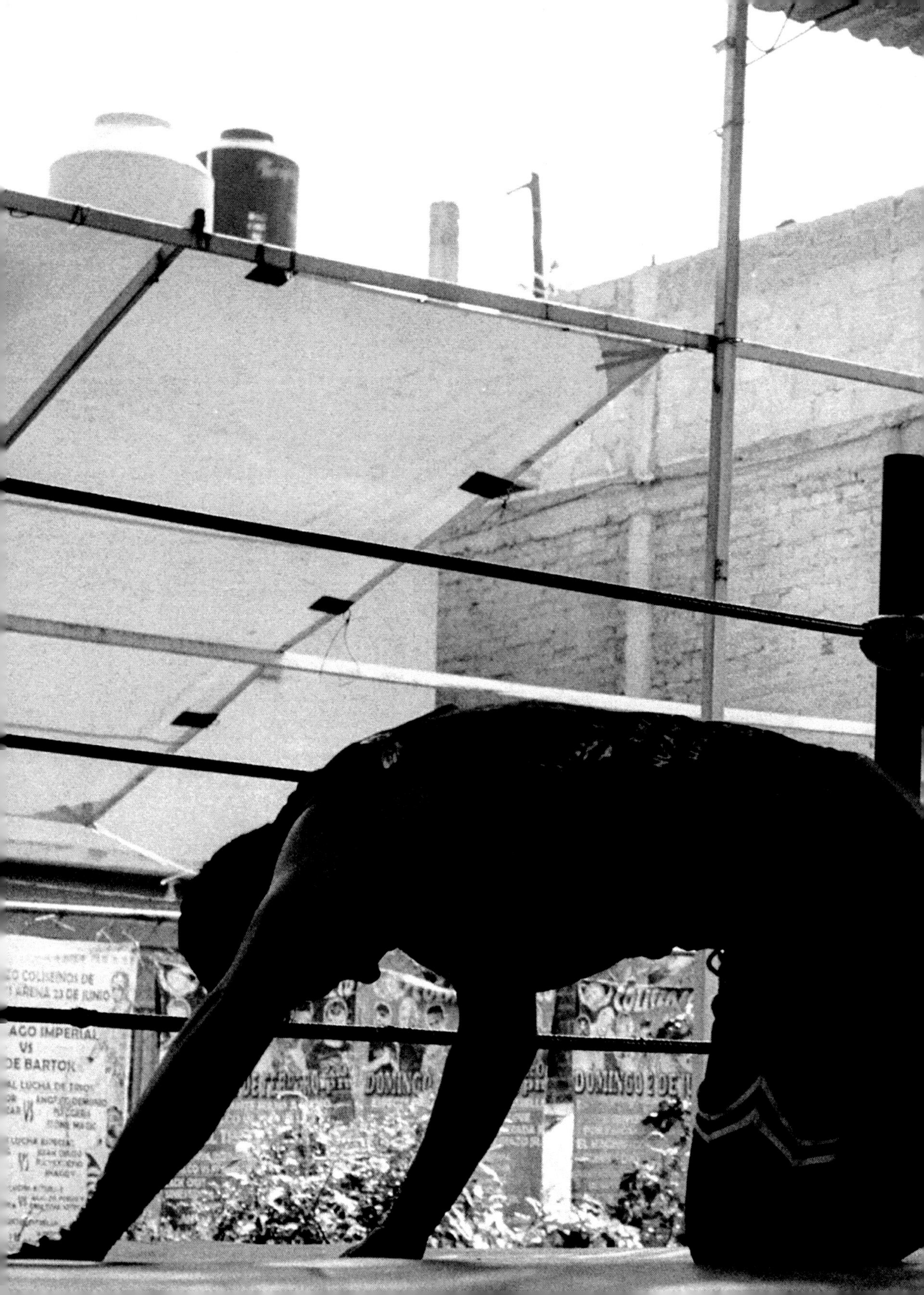

ACO IMPERIAL
VS
DE BARTOK
DOMINGO

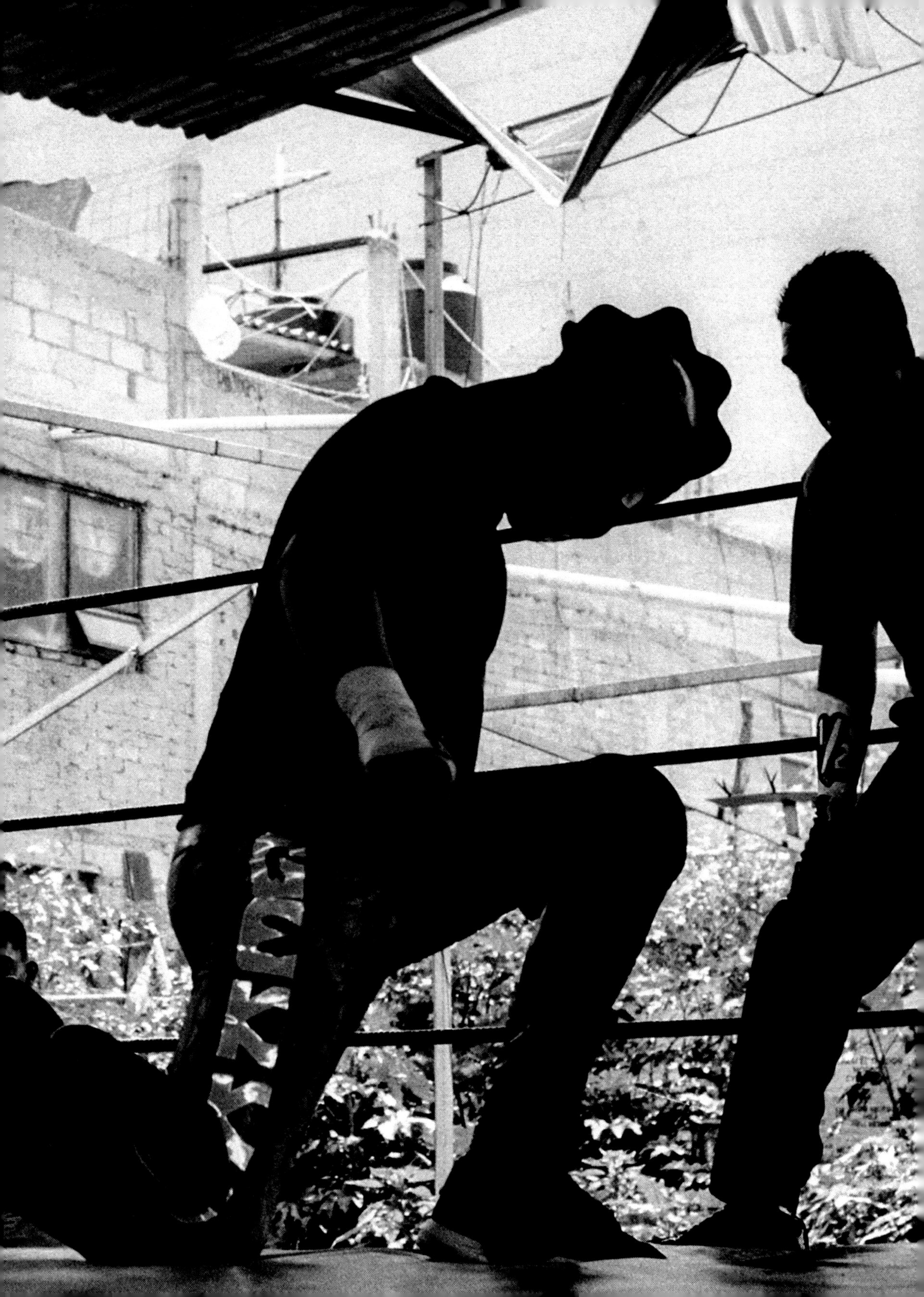

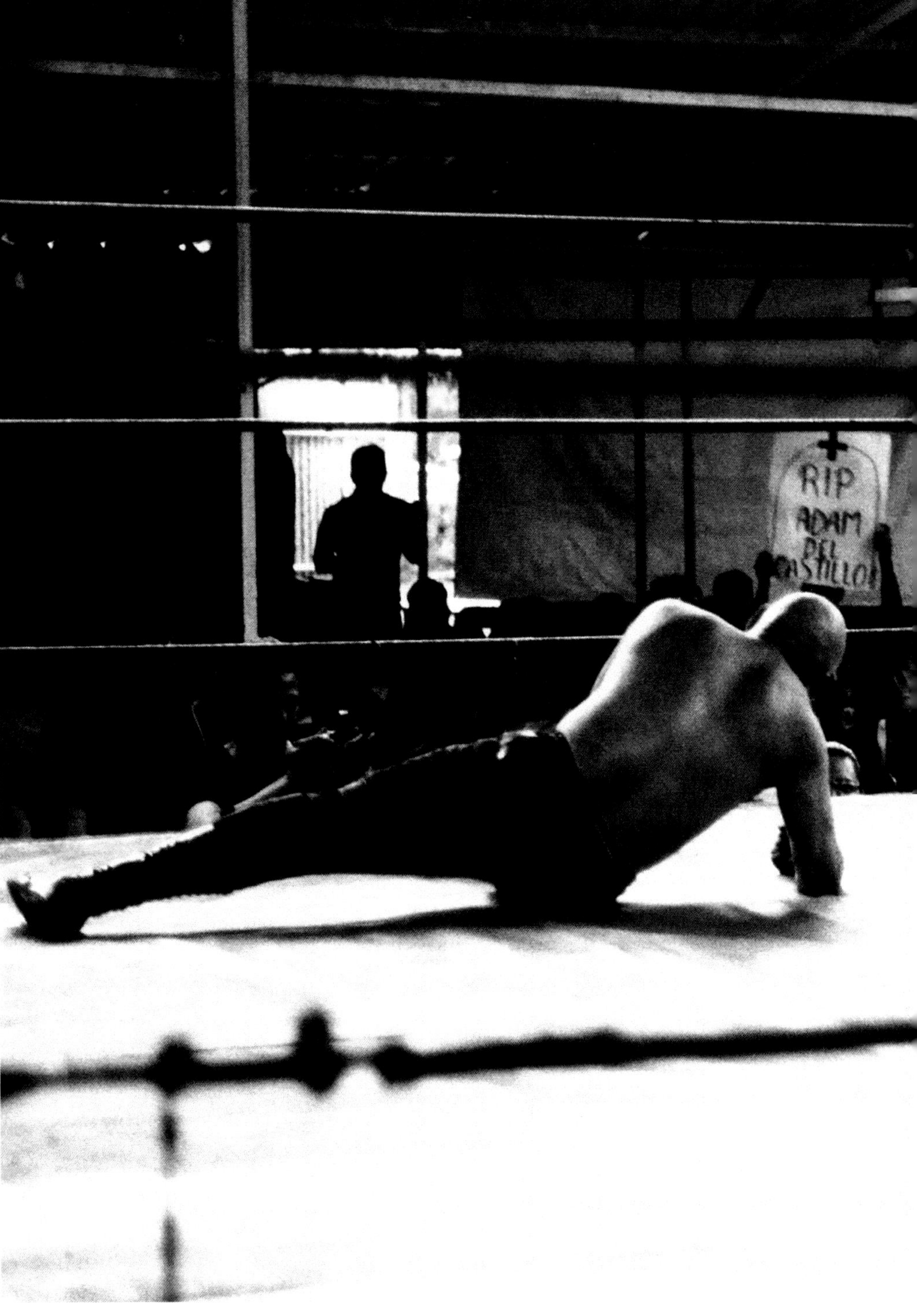
RIP
ADAM
DEL

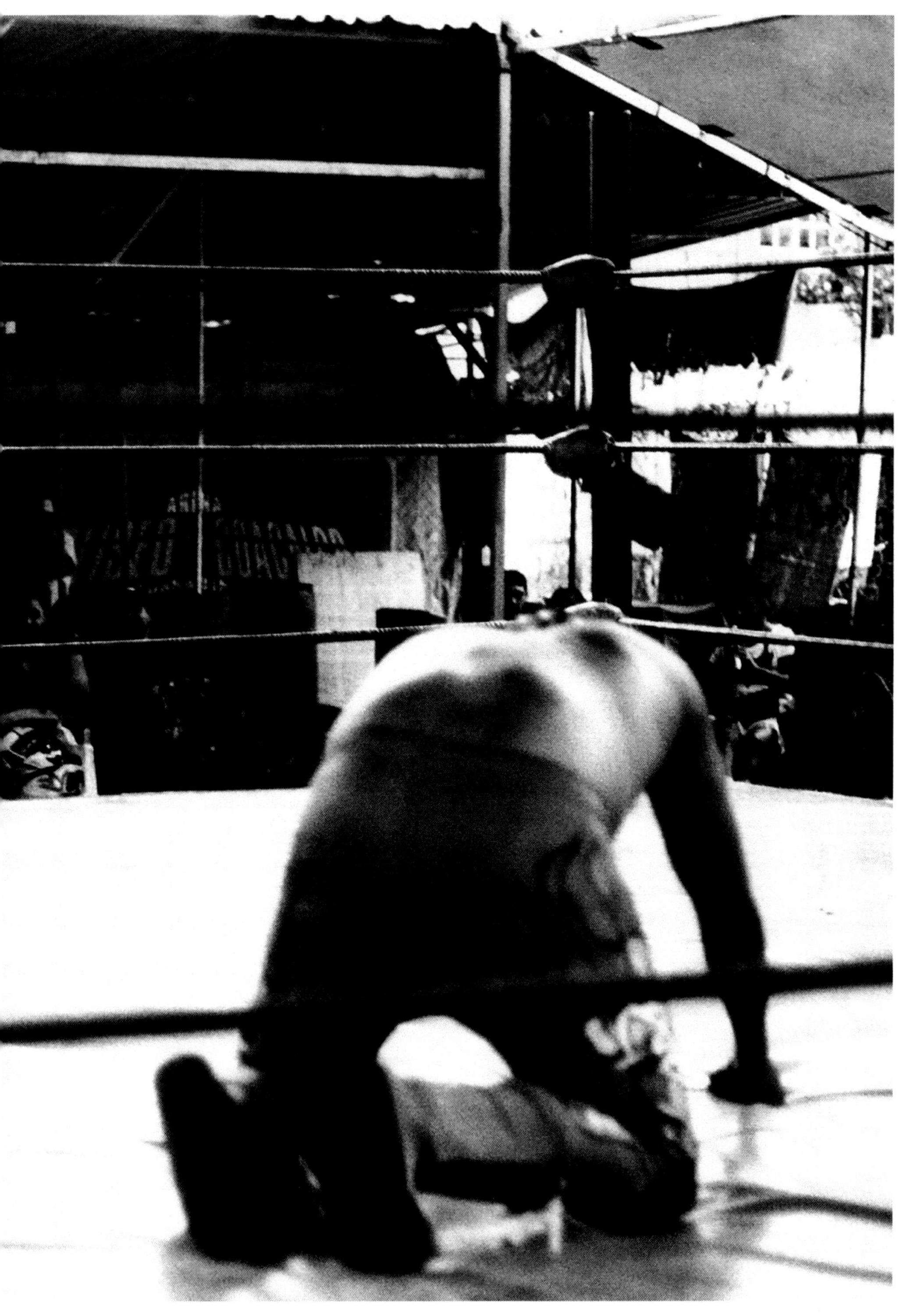

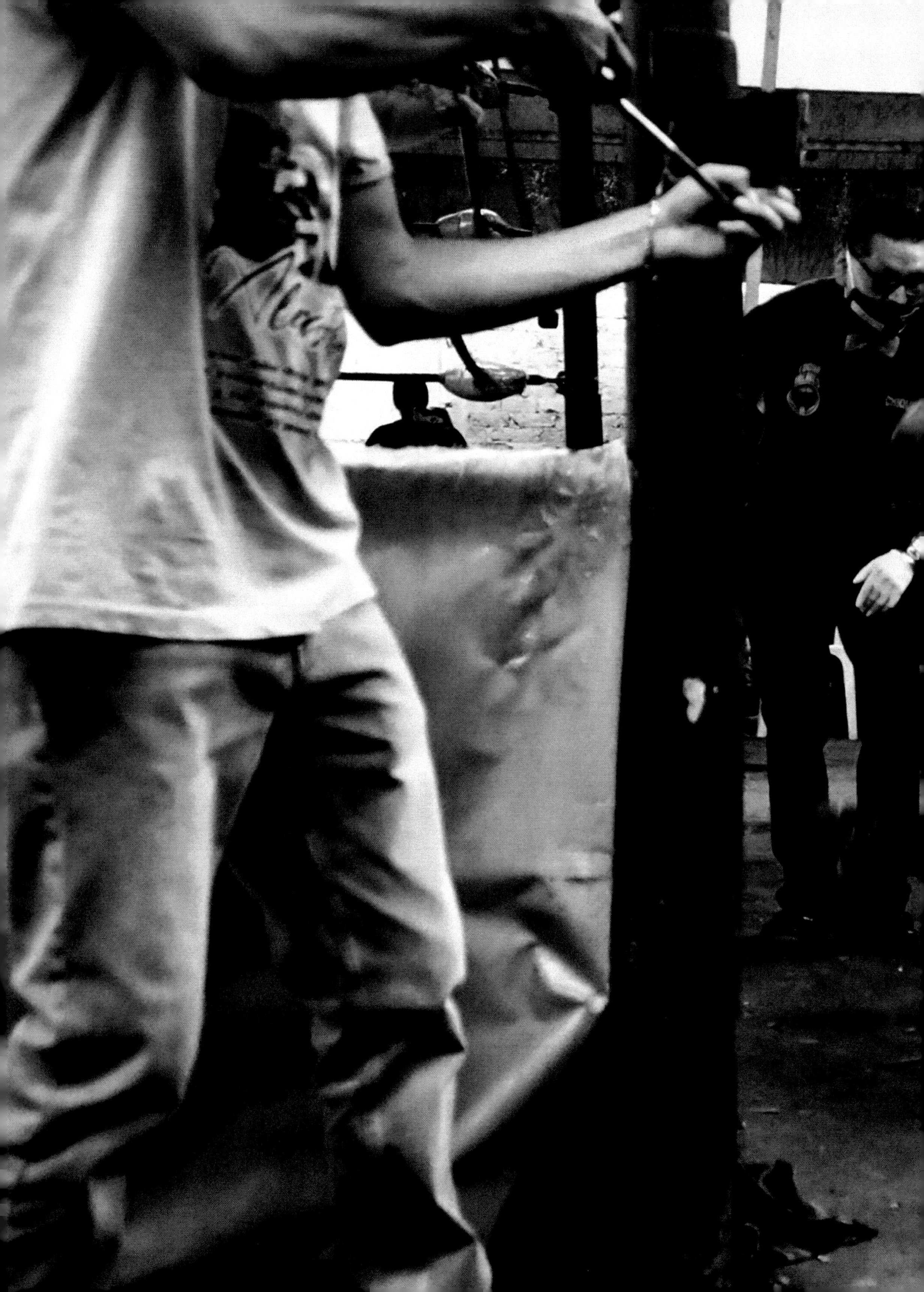

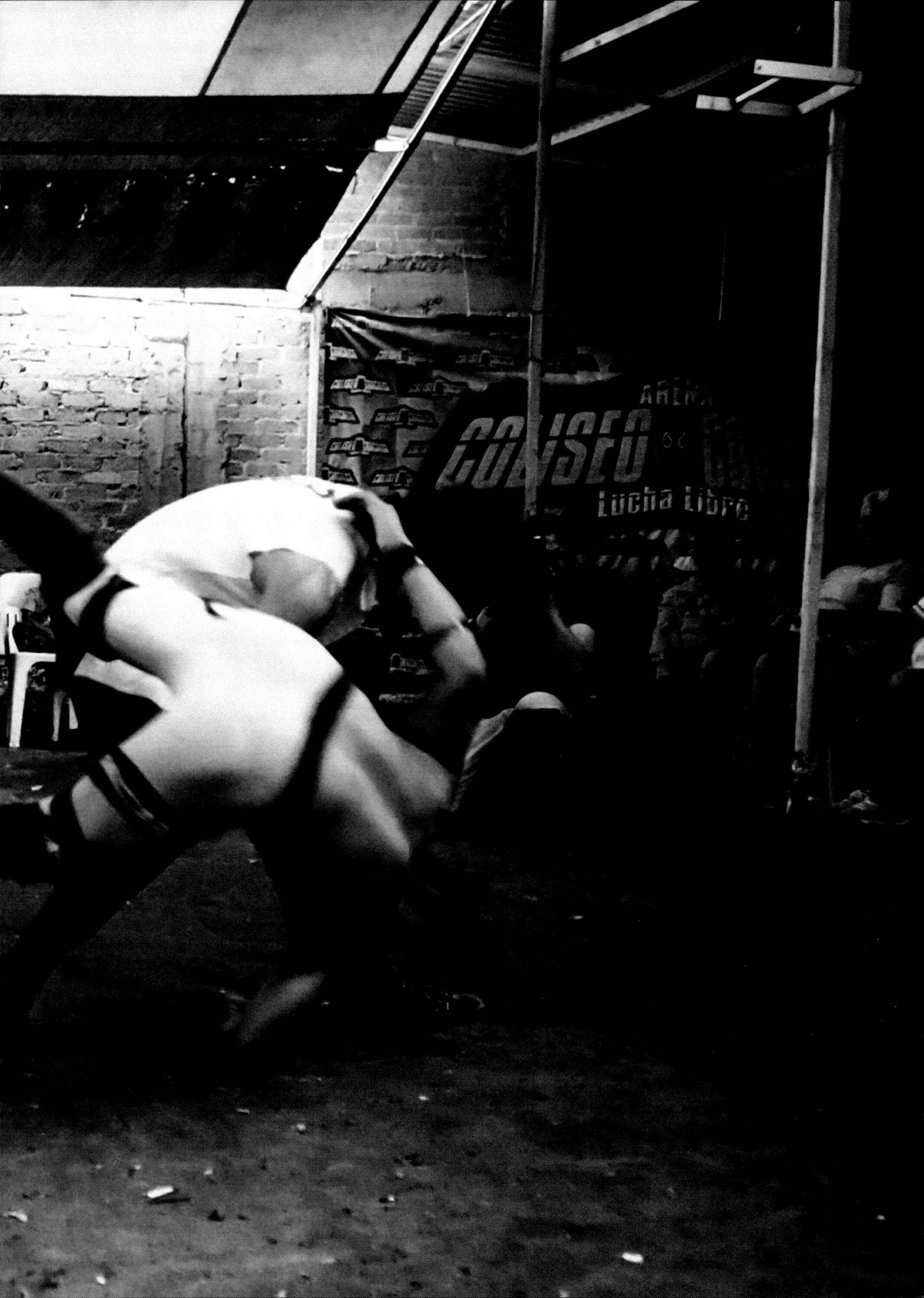
ARENA
COLISEO
Lucha Libre

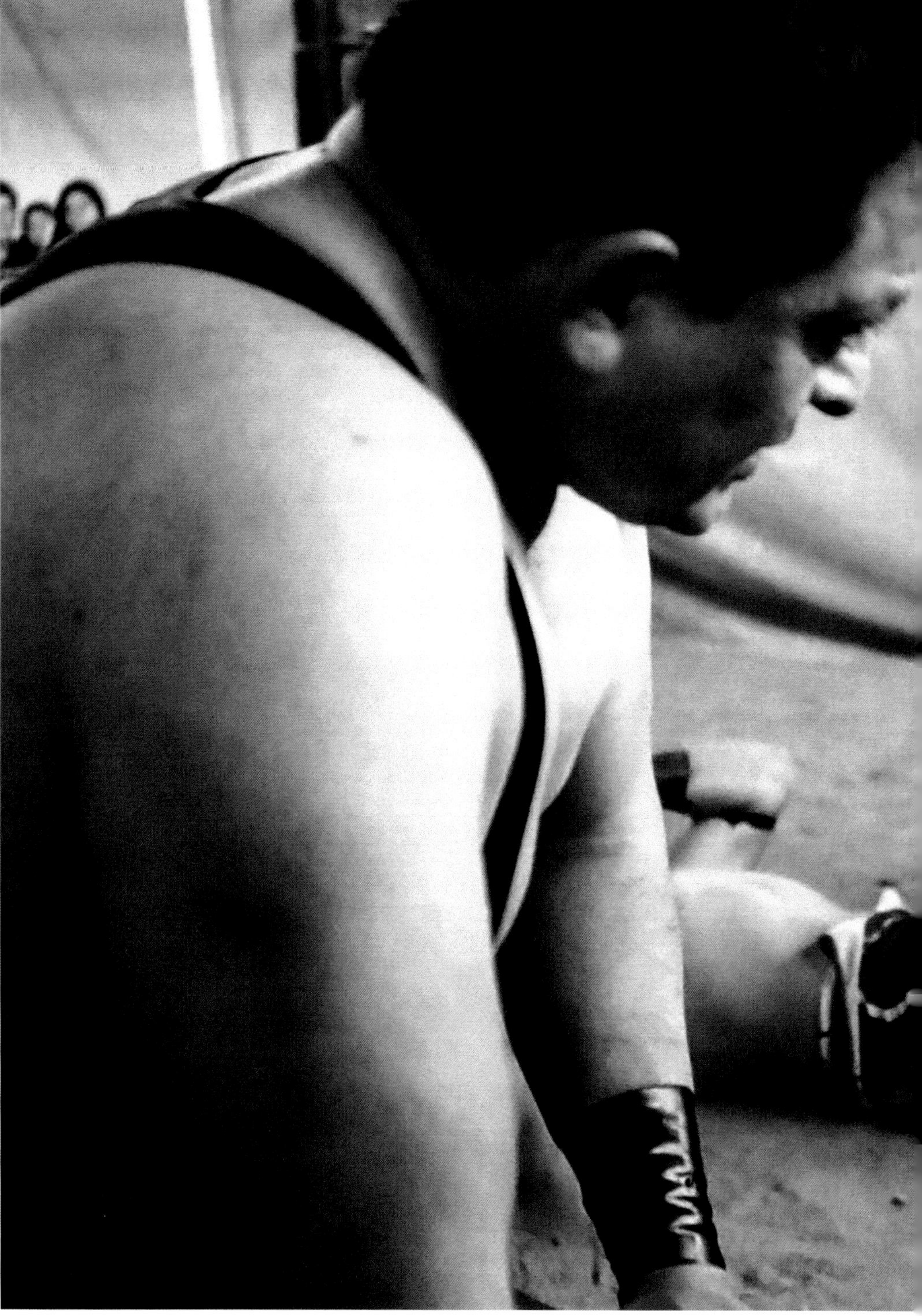

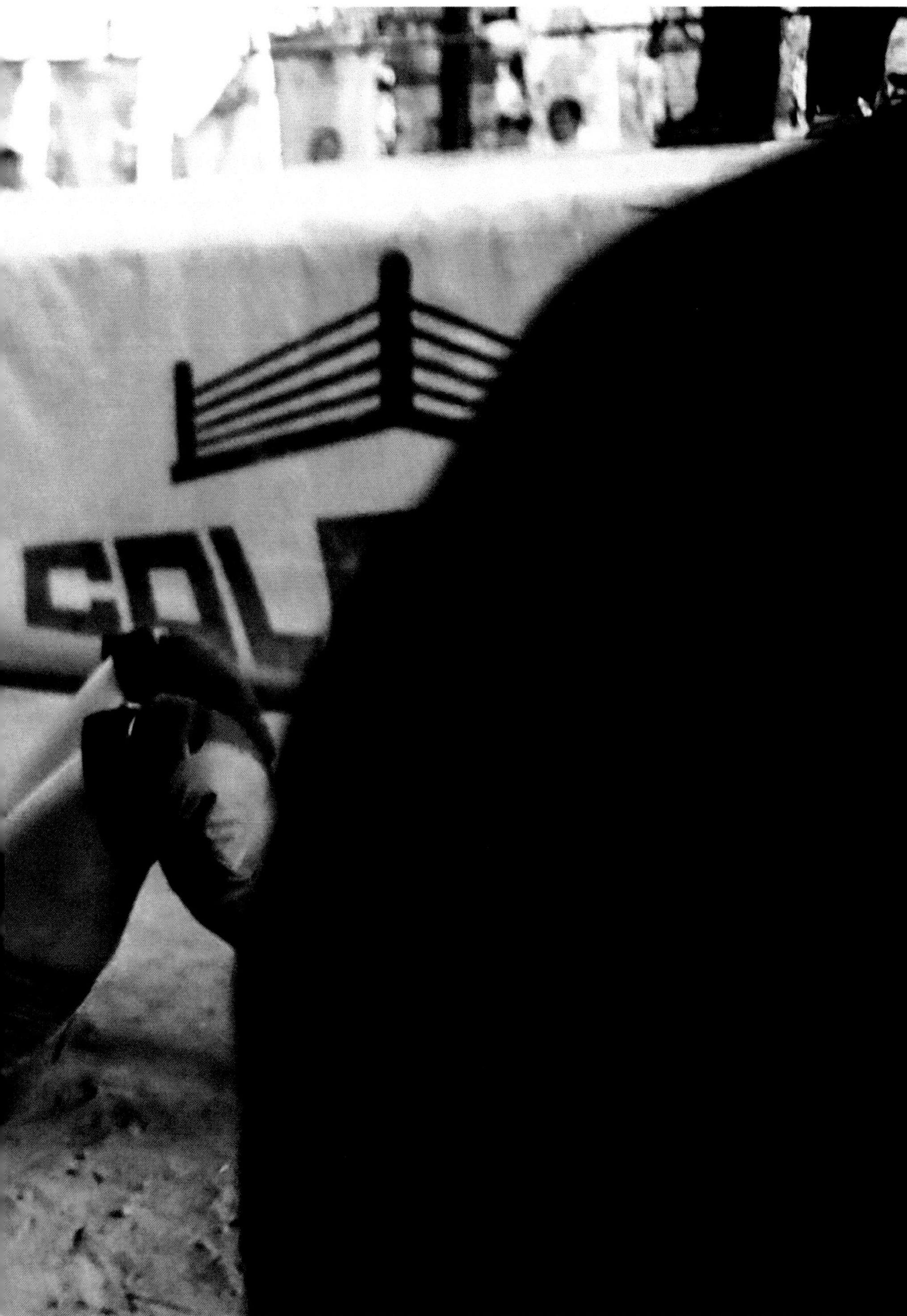

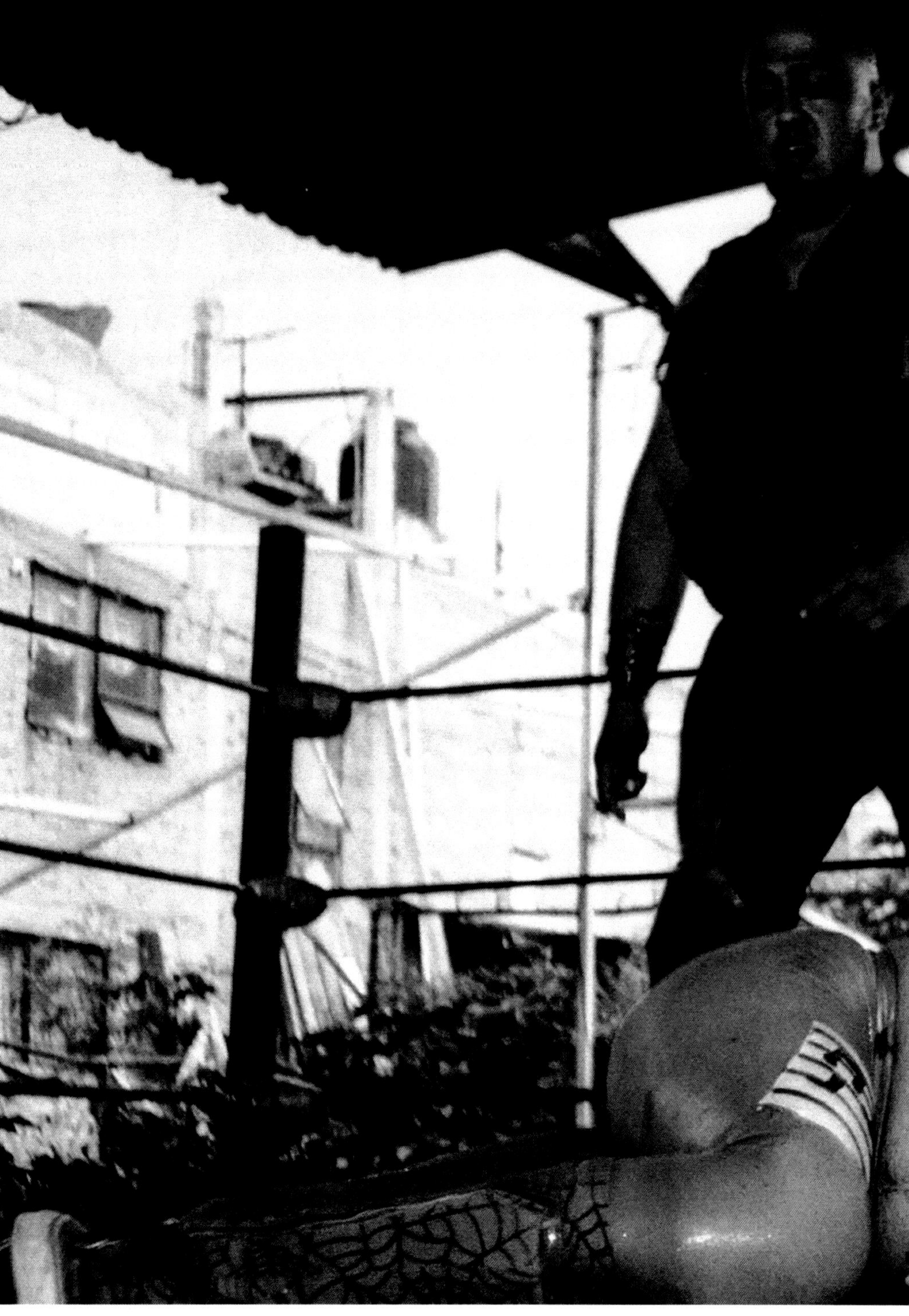

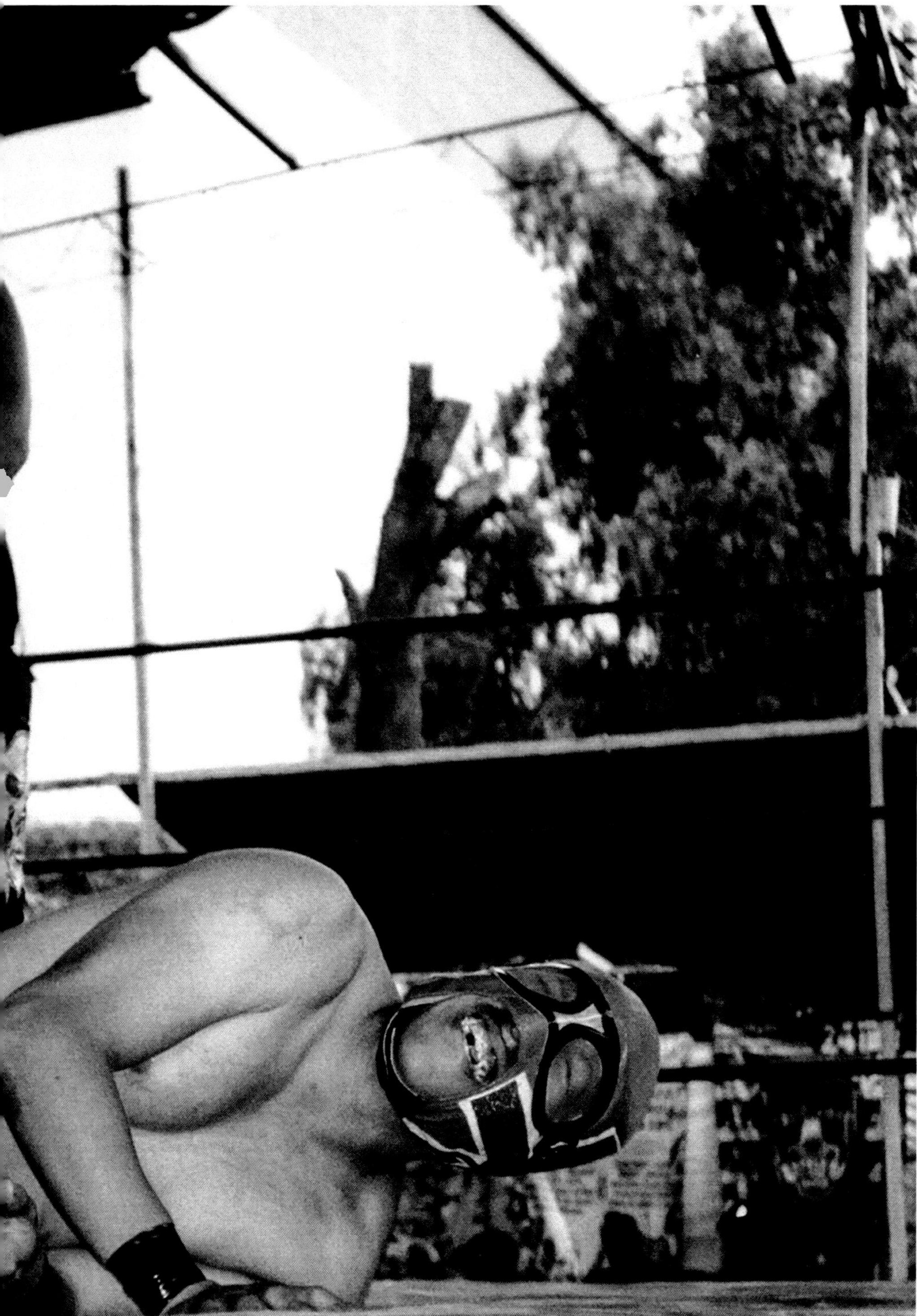

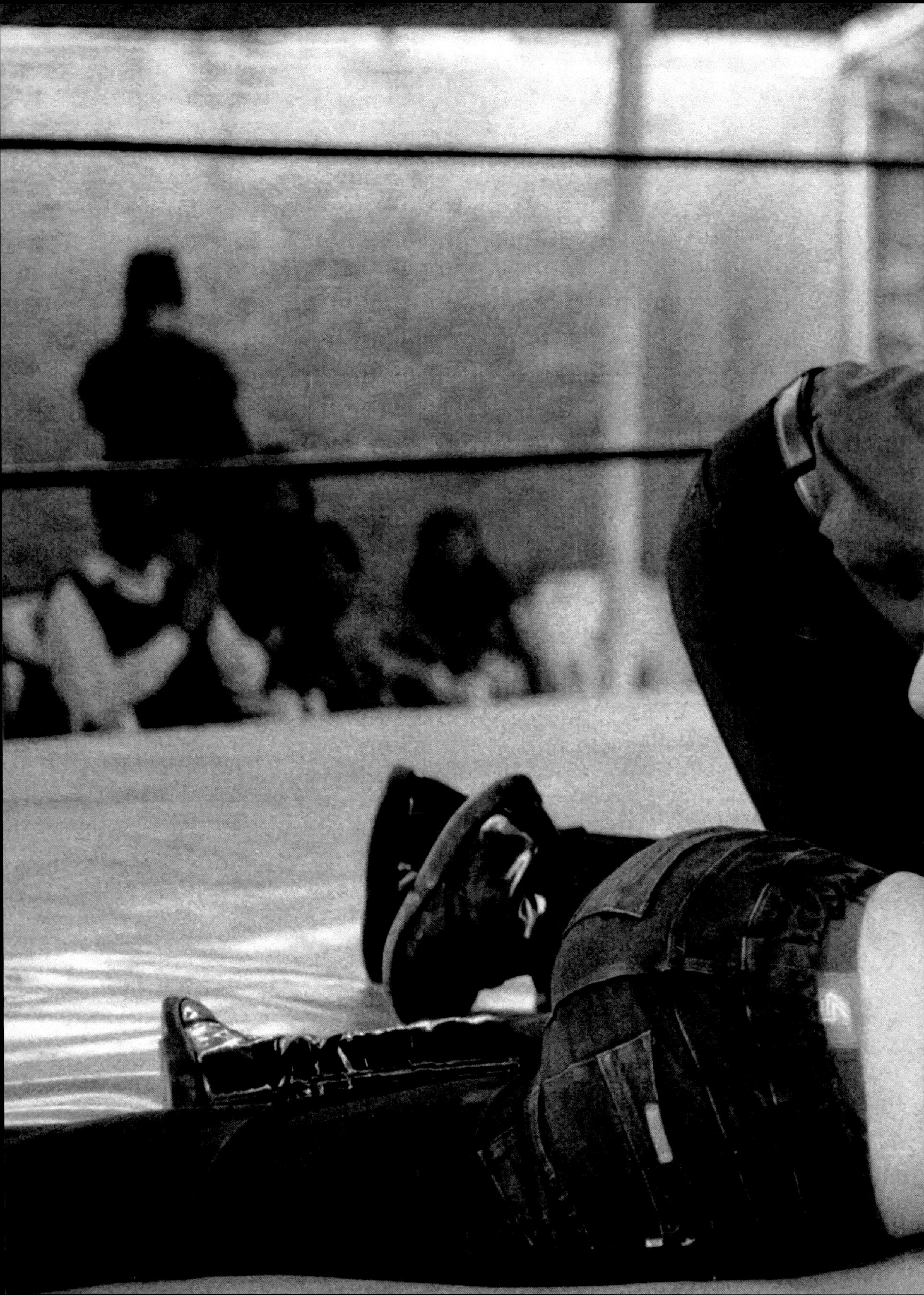

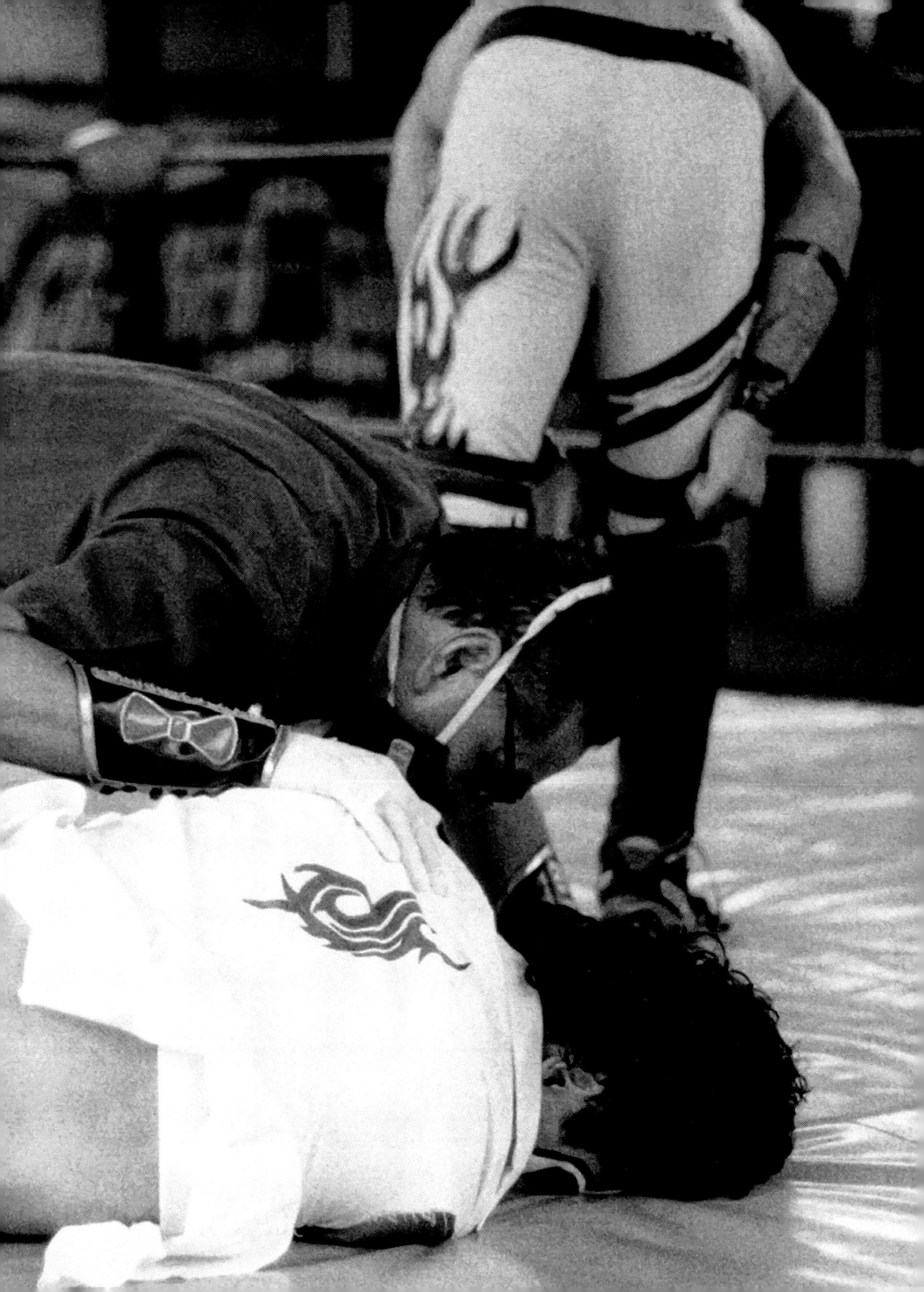

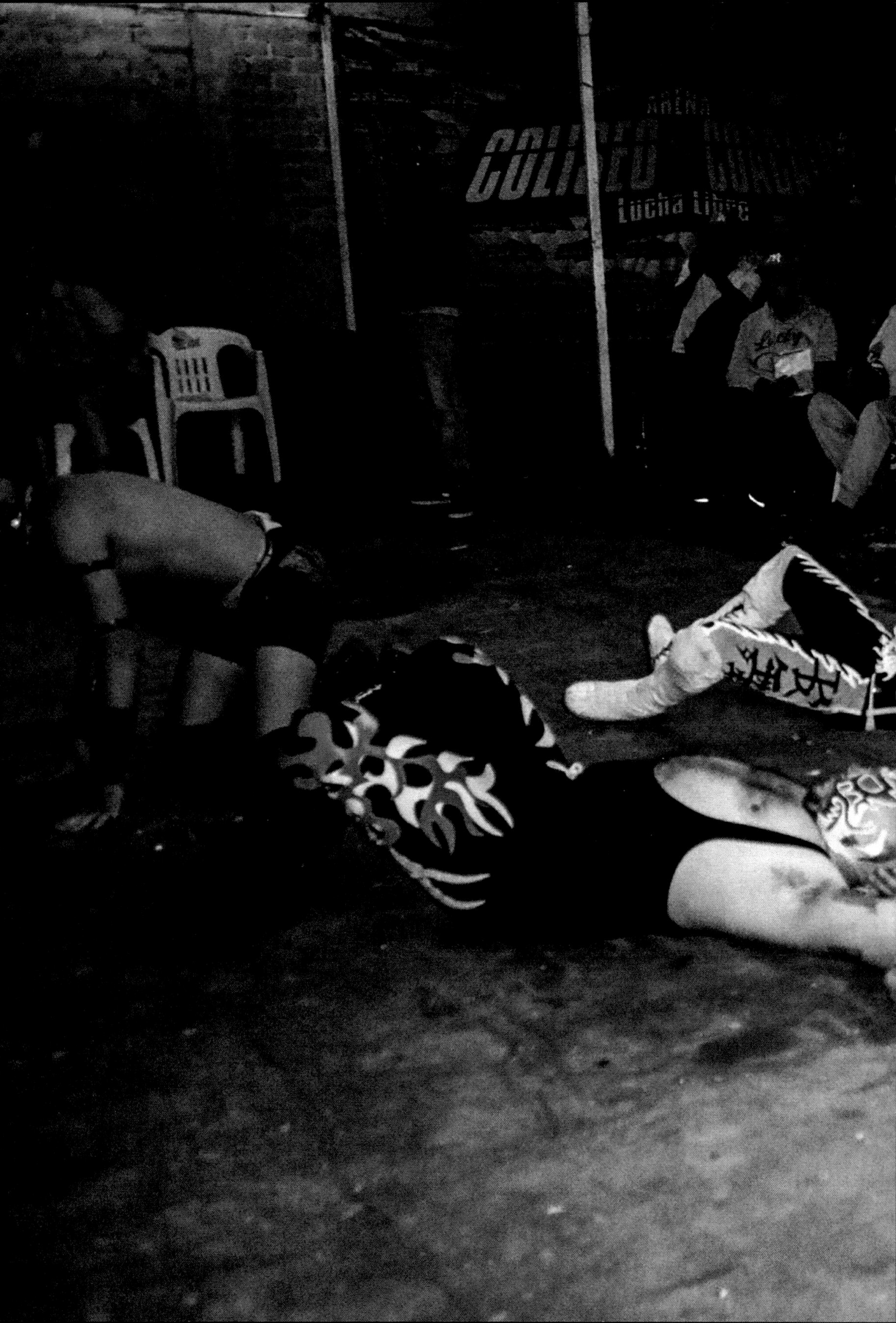
ARENA
COLISEO
Lucha Libre

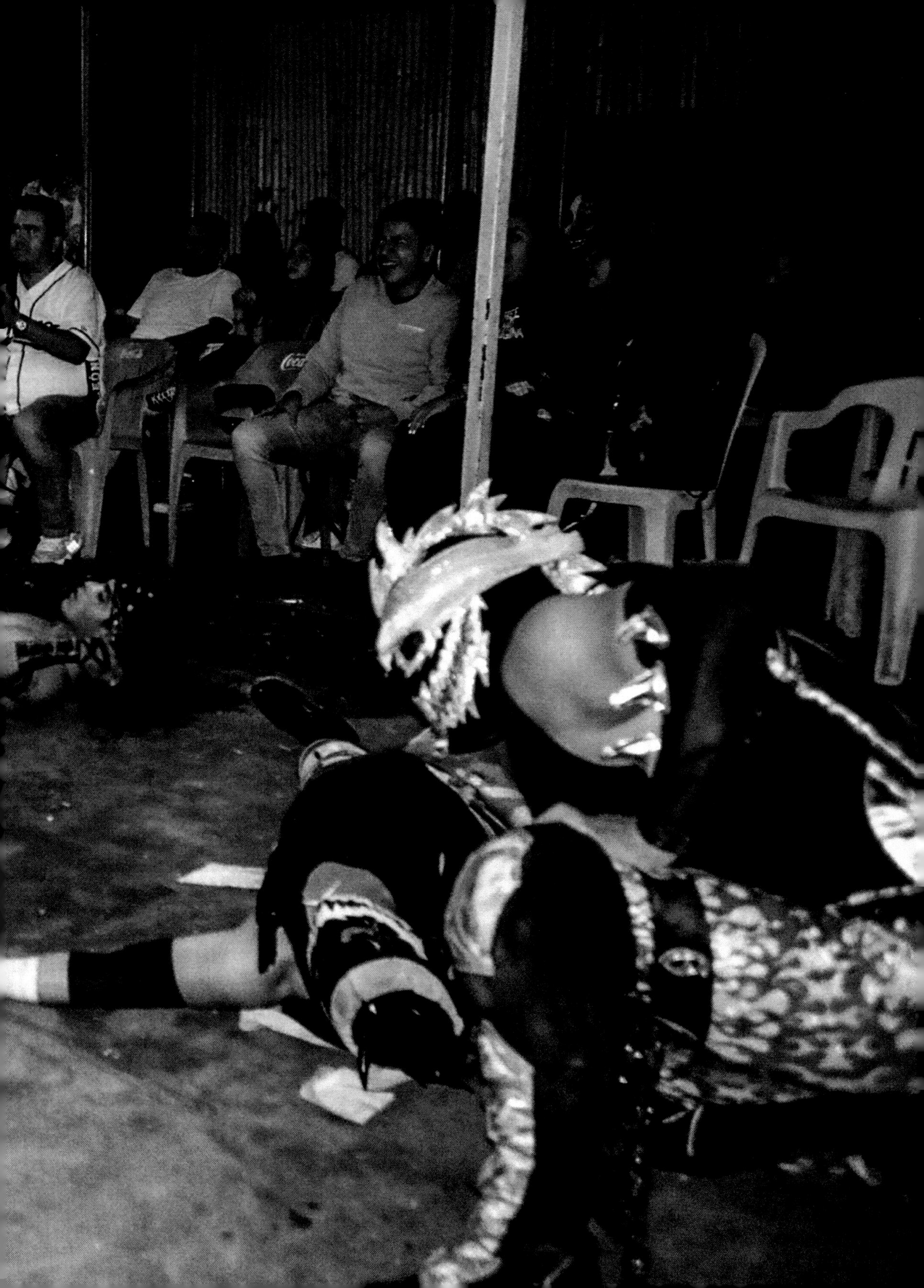

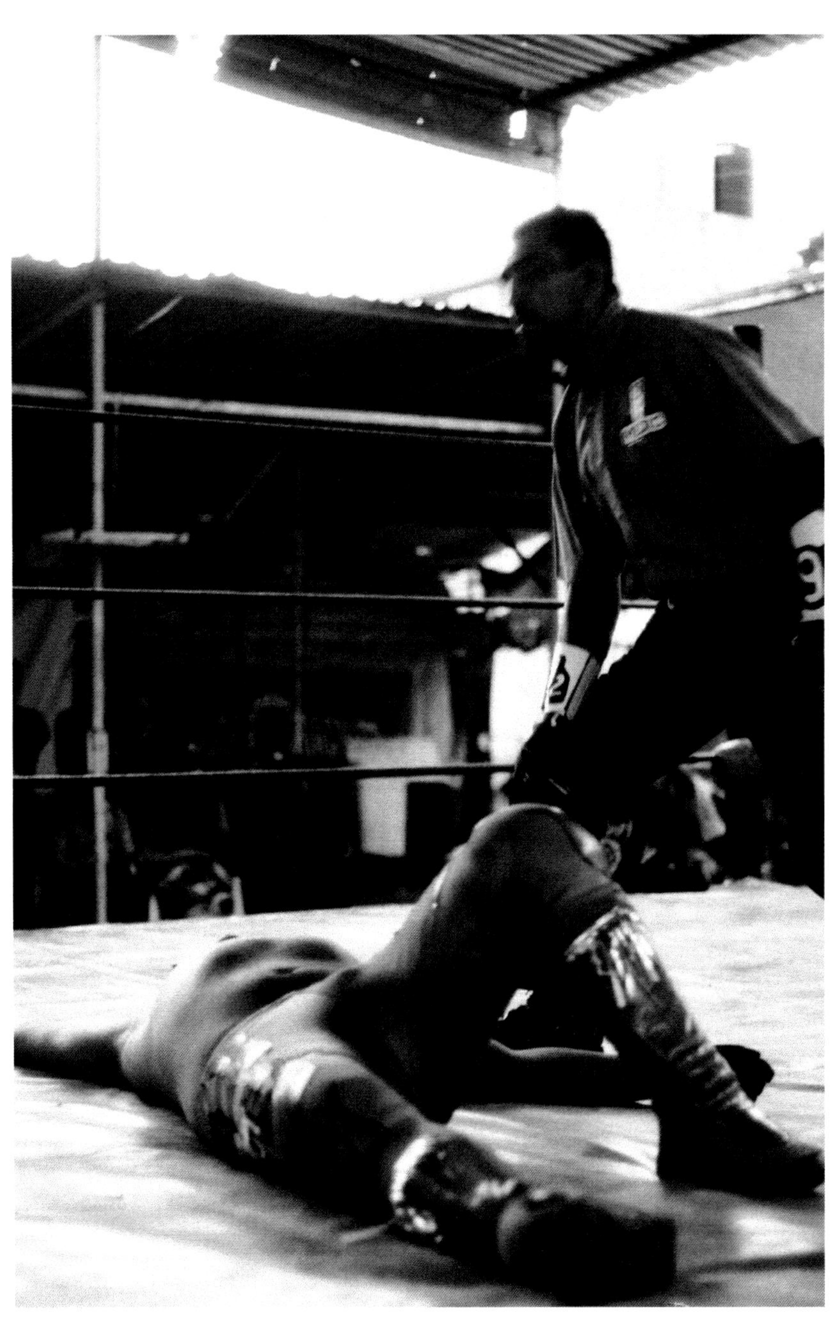

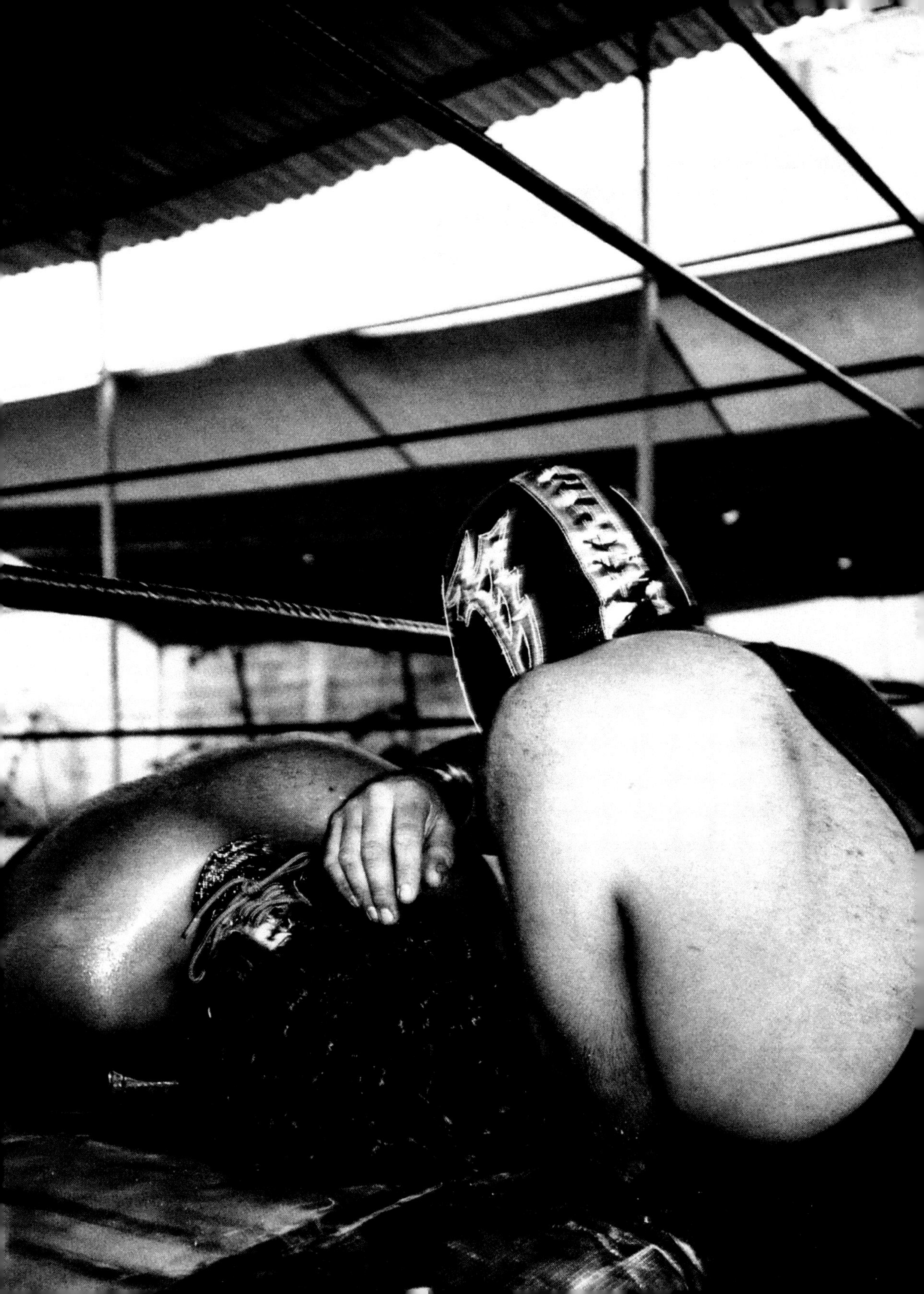

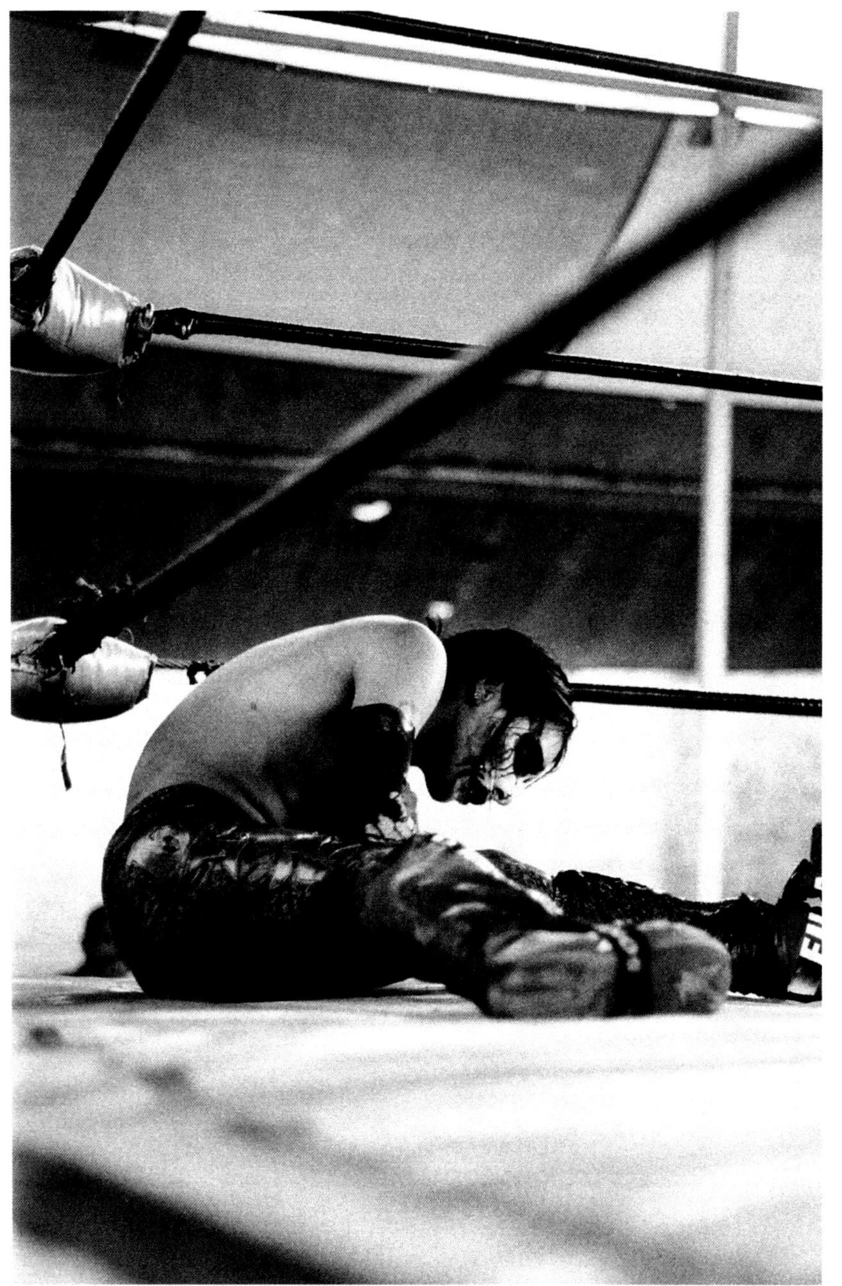

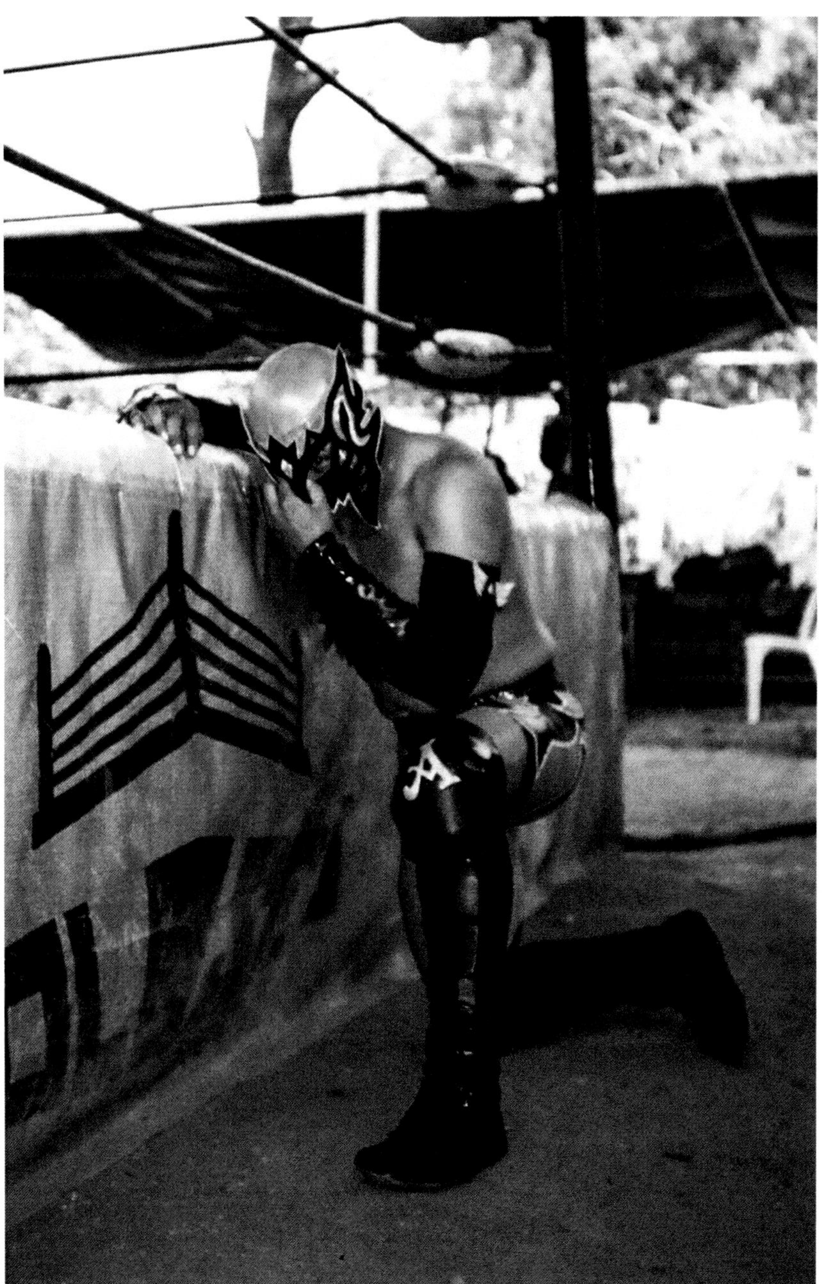

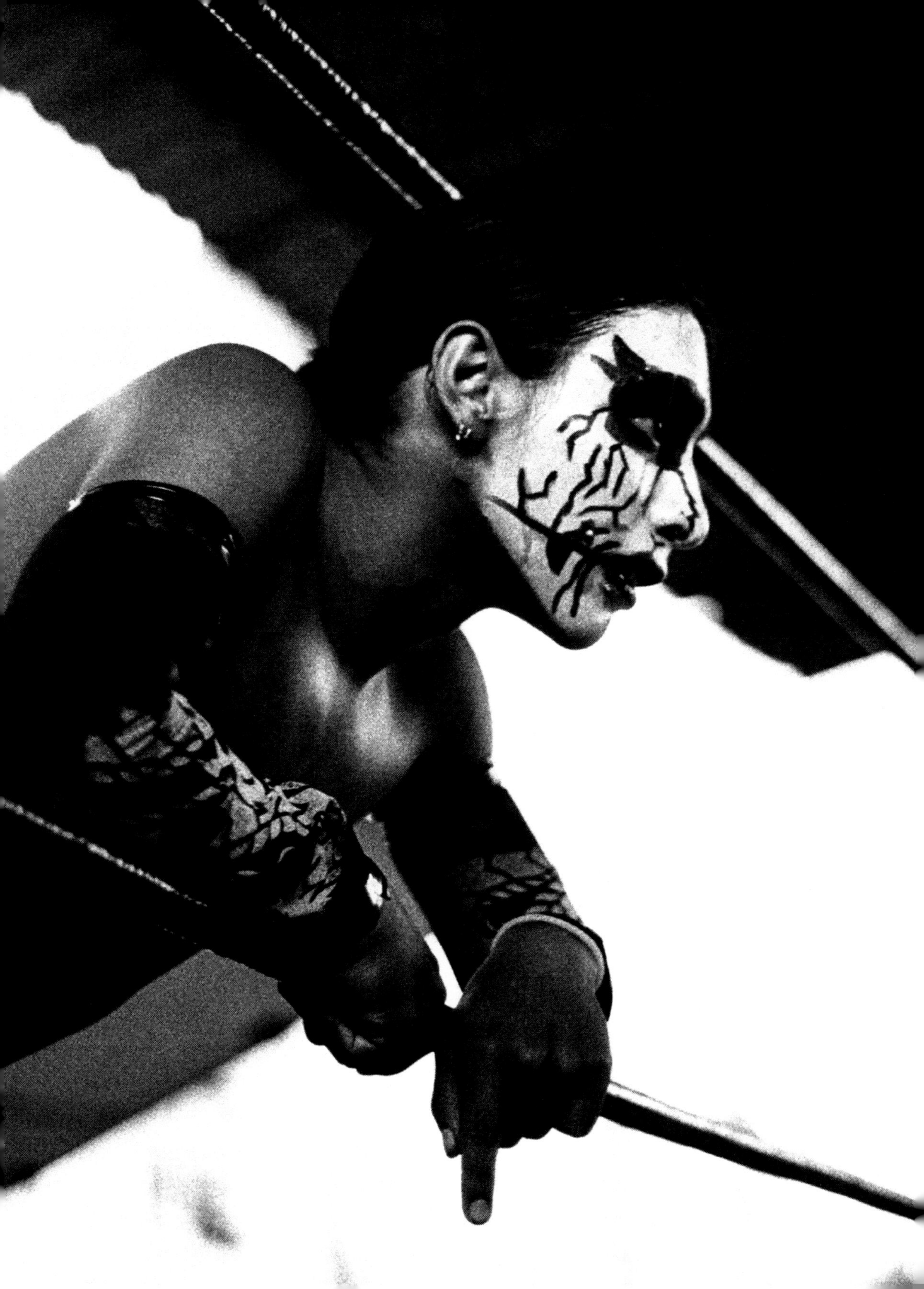

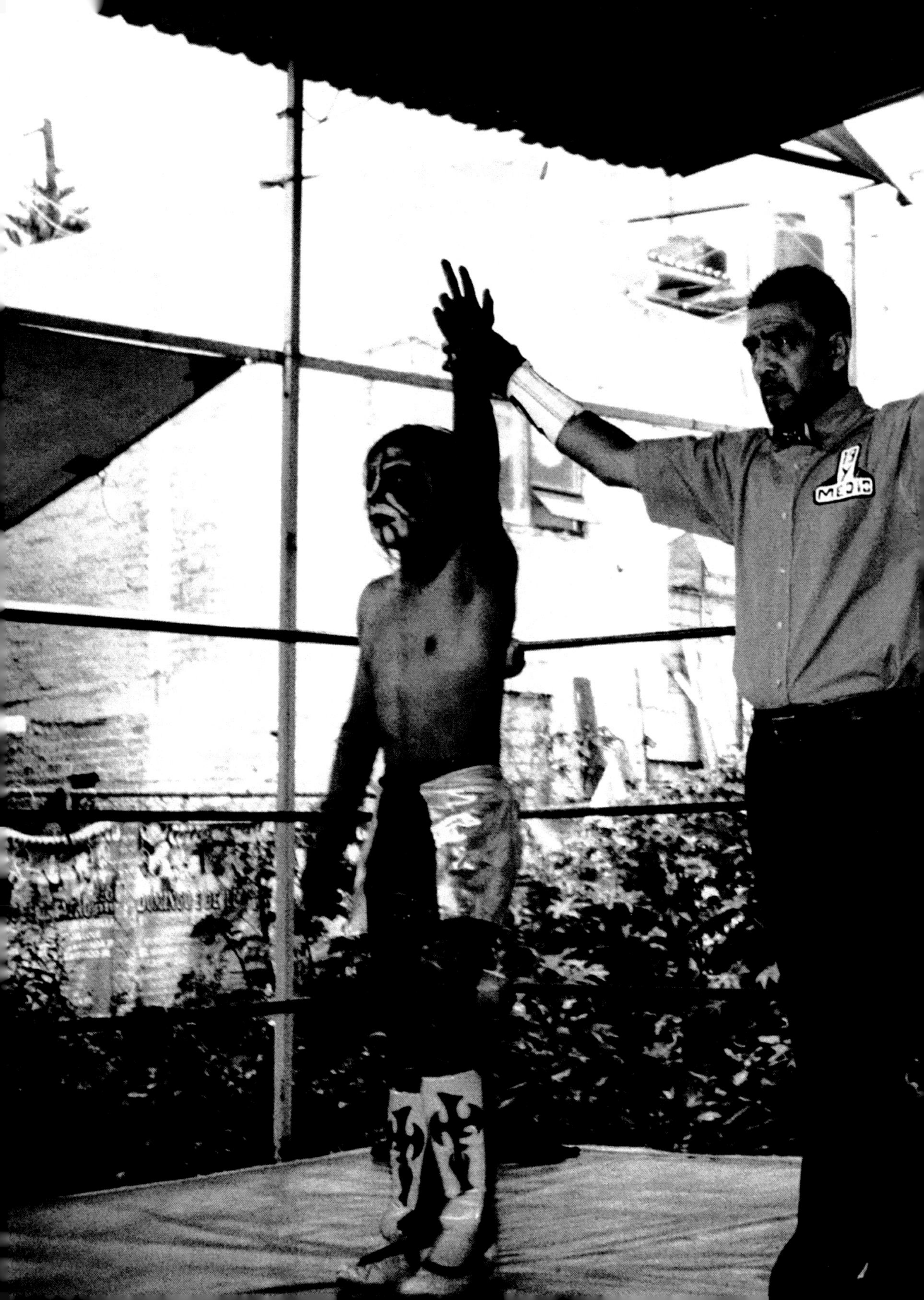
MEDIO

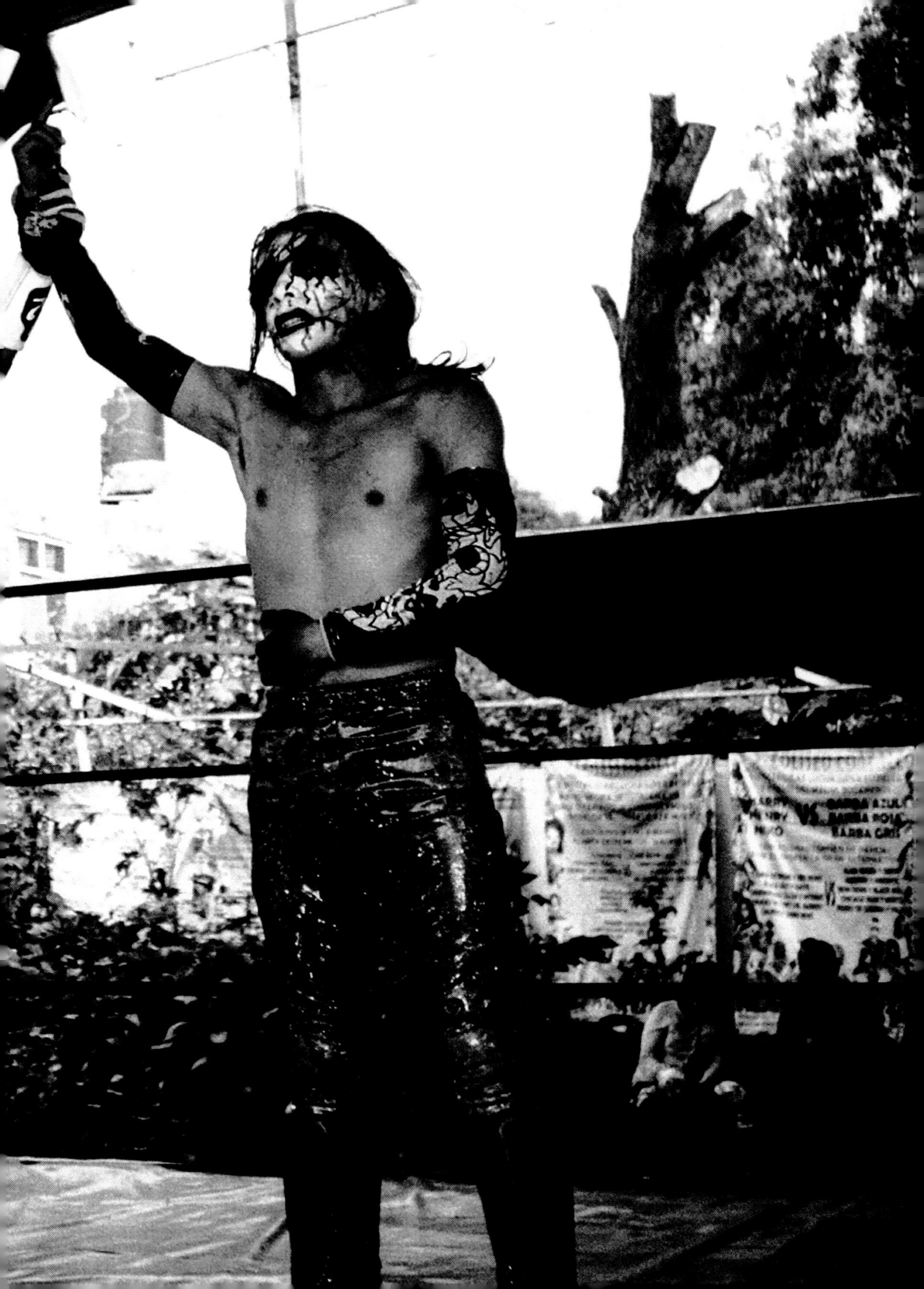
VS

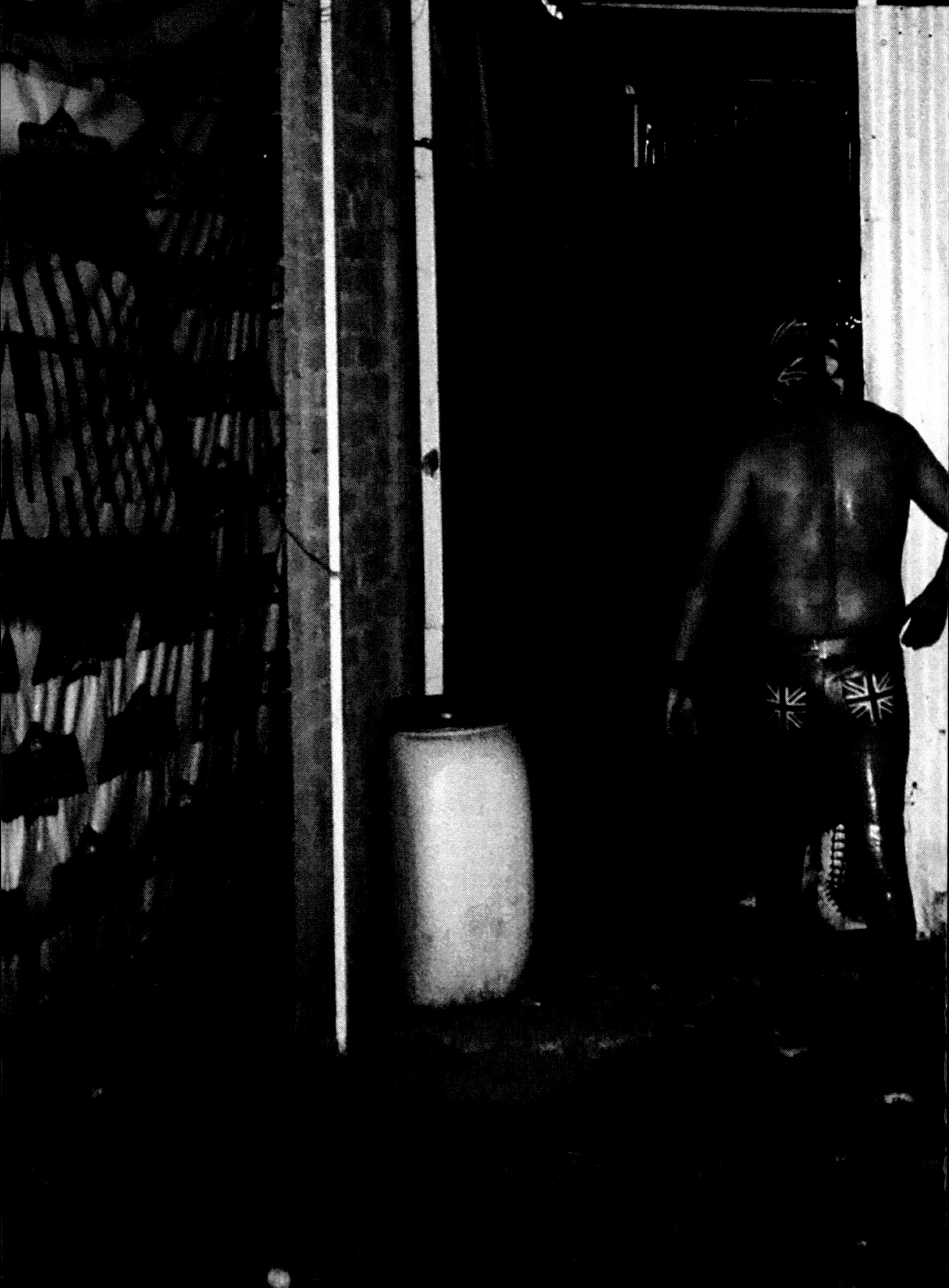

ISBN 978-1-963814-01-9

Printed in the U.K in a CarbonNeutral® facility

Design: Isla Anne Macmillan

Published by Blurring Books
BlurringBooks.com
@BlurringBooksNYC
Project management: Sean M. Johnson

The photography of Tyler Blint-Welsh (b.1996) is rooted in a curiosity and commitment to capturing truth, developed over years as a journalist for leading outlets including the Wall Street Journal, New York Times, and the Washington Post. Self-taught across of a range of analog formats, his work is the often result of the relationships he's formed – with luchadores in Mexico, global techno DJs, or pandemic-era medical workers – and reflects his deep desire to use storytelling as a means to understand the communities and subcultures that help shape our society. Blint-Welsh was born and raised in New York City, and works out of his studio in Brooklyn.

Number 10 in Blurring Books LSP Series
First Printing, Edition of 500

Blurring Books